Reading
and
Thinking
in English

**Concepts
in use**

Oxford
University
Press

Oxford University Press
Walton Street, Oxford OX2 6DP

London   New York   Toronto
Delhi   Bombay   Calcutta   Madras   Karachi
Kuala Lumpur   Singapore   Hong Kong   Tokyo
Nairobi   Dar es Salaam   Cape Town   Salisbury
Melbourne   Auckland

and associated companies in
Beirut   Berlin   Ibadan   Mexico City   Nicosia

OXFORD is a trademark of Oxford University Press

ISBN 0 19 451351 3

©The British Council 1980

First published 1980
Sixth impression 1985

Filmset by Keyspools Ltd. Golborne, Lancs.

Printed in Great Britain at the
University Press, Cambridge

Authors

Reading and Thinking in English was developed in a project sponsored jointly by the University of the Andes, Bogotá, Colombia, and the British Overseas Development Ministry in association with the British Council.

The Director of the project was John Moore, of the British Council, and the members of the University who participated in the writing of Concepts in Use were Beatriz Castilla de Campo, Carolina Muñoz de Marín, Claudia Lucía Ordóñez O, and Clara Helena Lobo-Guerrero de Saba.

Concepts in Use was revised and extended for publication in the Department of English as a Foreign Language of the University of London Institute of Education by John Moore, with the assistance of Teresa Munévar from the University of the Andes.

Professor H. G. Widdowson (of the University of London Institute of Education) is the Associate Editor of Reading and Thinking in English.

Reading and Thinking in English

Reading and Thinking in English is an integrated course in reading comprehension for students of English as a foreign language. It is based on the belief that a special kind of course is required for students of English whose main need is to gain access to information through English. The course has been designed for a wide range of learners whose needs can be described as 'English for Academic Purposes'—secondary school pupils, students in universities and other tertiary institutions, adults whose profession requires them to make use of material in English. It is therefore intended to help students and others read textbooks, works of reference and general academic interest, sourcebooks and journals in English.

The series consists of four books. **Concepts in use** extends students' basic knowledge of grammar and vocabulary and how they are used to express fundamental concepts. It also develops their awareness of how passages are built on combinations of these concepts. **Exploring functions** deals with the use of concepts in the communicative functions of academic writing. **Discovering discourse** develops students' awareness of how the devices of language are used to express communicative function. It also shows how passages are built on combinations of simple functions. **Discourse in action** extends students' knowledge of the functional organization of written English and develops their ability to handle information found in varied types of real academic discourse. The series is designed so that the books in it can be used independently of the others in the series. Many intermediate or advanced learners may be able to begin with the third or fourth books. The whole series, however, provides a phased approach to the most challenging demands of academic discourse.

Contents

Unit 1   Systems

The solar system

DIAGRAM

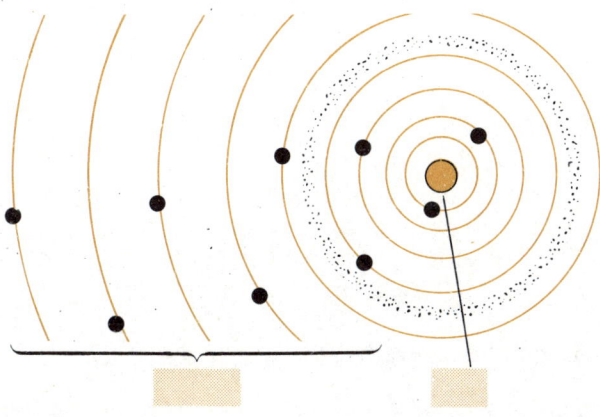

SUMMARY

SYSTEM	PARTS
the solar system	the sun the planets

STATEMENTS
The sun is the centre of the solar system.
There are nine planets in the solar system.
The solar system consists of the sun and nine planets.

Task 1   Label the diagram.

The atom

DIAGRAM

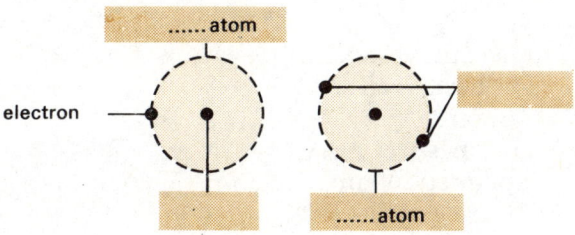

1

SUMMARY

SYSTEM	PARTS
the atom	the nucleus

STATEMENTS
An atom is a system.
An atom consists of a nucleus and one or more electrons.
The nucleus is the centre of the atom.
There are two electrons in a helium atom.
There is one electron in a hydrogen atom.

Task 2   Label the diagrams.

Task 3   Complete the summary.

Part 2
Language study

Patterns 1	*The atom is a system.*

Task 4   Match the members and classes. For example, 1e.

	MEMBER		CLASS
1	Jupiter and Venus	a	instrument
2	the heart	b	machine
3	carbon	c	element
4	the thermometer	d	organ
5	turbines	e	planet
6	hydrogen	f	gas

Task 5   Complete these statements.
1   The heart is an . . . . . .
2   Carbon . . . . . .
3   Turbines are . . . . . .
4   Jupiter and Venus . . . . . .
5   . . . . . . a gas.

2

6   Thermometers . . . . . .
7   A turbine . . . . . .
8   . . . . . . a planet.

Task 6   Correct these statements.

EXAMPLE: Turbines are organs.
CORRECTION: Turbines are machines.

1   Carbon is a gas.
2   Thermometers are elements.
3   An organ is the heart.
4   Planets are Jupiter and Venus.

Patterns 2

| The solar system | consists of | the sun and nine planets. |
| The atom | | the nucleus and one or more electrons. |

Task 7   Match the systems and parts.

SYSTEM		PARTS	
1	the solar system	a	the brain, the spinal cord, the nerves
2	a carbon atom	b	the nucleus, six electrons
3	the cell	c	the sun, nine planets
4	the nervous system	d	the nucleus, the cytoplasm
5	an ecosystem	e	organisms, their environment
6	the cardio-vascular system	f	the heart, the blood vessels

Task 8   Complete these statements.
1   The carbon atom consists of . . . . . . and . . . . . .
2   The cell consists of . . . . . .
3   The cardio-vascular system . . . . . .
4   . . . . . . consists of organisms and their environment.
5   . . . . . . the brain, the spinal cord and . . . . . .

Task 9   Correct these statements.

EXAMPLE: The solar system consists of the nucleus and one or more electrons.

3

CORRECTION: The solar system consists of the sun and the planets.
OR: The atom consists of the nucleus and one or more electrons.

1   The cell consists of organisms and their environment.
2   The carbon atom consists of the nucleus and two electrons.
3   The heart and the blood vessels consist of the cardio-vascular system.
4   The brain, the spinal cord and the nerves consist of the nervous system.

Patterns 3

The nucleus is the centre of the atom.
= The centre of the atom is the nucleus.
= The centre of the atom is called the nucleus.

Task 10

Match the names and descriptions.

	NAME		DESCRIPTION
1	spine	a	centre of the eye
2	photosphere	b	metric unit of force
3	pupil	c	composition of metals
4	gramme	d	centre of the skeleton
5	Newton	e	surface of the sun
6	alloy	f	metric unit of mass

Task 11

Complete these statements.
1   The spine . . . . . .
2   The Newton . . . . . .
3   . . . . . . the centre of the eye.
4   . . . . . . the surface of the sun.
5   The metric unit of mass is called the . . . . . .
6   A composition of metals . . . . . . an alloy.
7   The centre of the skeleton . . . . . .
8   . . . . . . the gramme.

Part 3
Discourse study

Class-member relations

Task 12

Selecting information
Read the passage and complete table 1.

4

THE SOLAR SYSTEM

The solar system consists of a star (the sun), the planets and a number of other bodies, such as satellites and asteroids. The sun is the centre of the solar system. The planets revolve around it. There are nine planets in all. They are as follows: Mercury, Venus, Earth, Mars, Jupiter, Saturn, Uranus, Neptune and Pluto. Some planets have satellites. The Earth has one satellite. It is called the Moon.

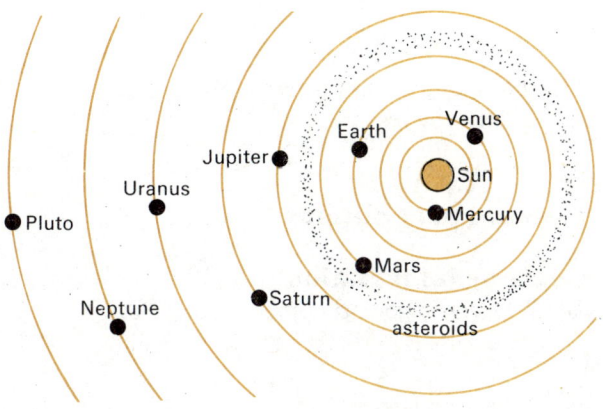

TABLE 1

planets	Mercury
	Neptune

Task 13

Presenting information
Use table 2 to complete the passage.

TABLE 2

Main parts of a complex plant	roots stem flower leaves

There are . . . . . . main parts of a . . . . as follows : the roots . . . . . . and the leaves.

System-part relations

Task 14

Selecting information
Read the passage and complete table 3.

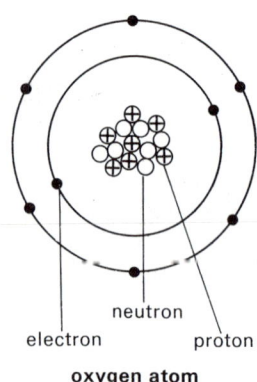

neutron
electron   proton
oxygen atom

THE ATOM
The atom is a system. It consists of a nucleus and one or more electrons. The nucleus is the centre of the atom and consists of protons and neutrons. The electrons move around the central nucleus.

There is only one electron in the hydrogen atom. There are seven electrons in the nitrogen atom and eight in the oxygen atom. An atom of iron contains twenty-six electrons.

TABLE 3

ELEMENT	NUMBER OF ELECTRONS IN AN ATOM
hydrogen	
	7

Task 15

Presenting information
Use table 4 to complete the passage.

TABLE 4

TYPE OF NERVE	NUMBER
peripheral	43 pairs
cranial	12 pairs
spinal	31 pairs

The peripheral nervous system consists of a number of different nerves.
There are ...... of peripheral nerves and 31 pairs of ...... There are
also ......

**Part 4
Extension**

Task 16

Read the passage and label the diagram.

INSECT ANATOMY
The body of an insect consists of three main parts: the head, the thorax
and the abdomen. The head contains the insect's brain, eyes and mouth.
It also carries the antennae. The thorax is the central part of the body. It
bears the legs and wings. There are three pairs of legs and two pairs of
wings. The insect's abdomen contains its digestive and reproductive
organs.

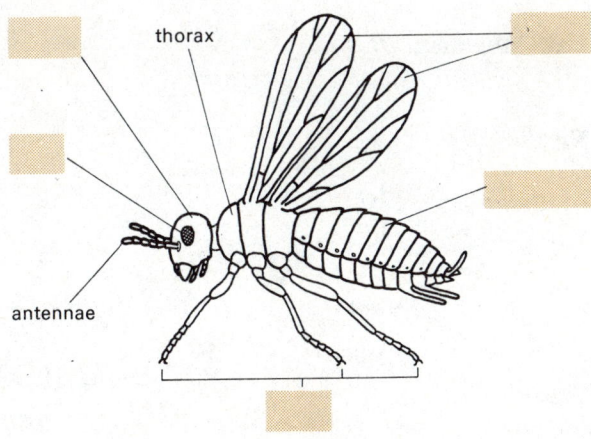

thorax

antennae

Unit 2   States of systems

Part 1
Presentation

Mars

DIAGRAM

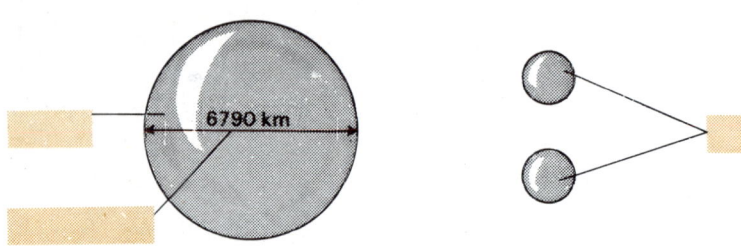

SUMMARY

SYSTEM	CHARACTERISTICS	
Mars	diameter	6790 km
	number of satellites	2
	life	none
	maximum temperature	$-22°C$

STATEMENTS
Mars is a planet.
It has two small satellites.
Its diameter is 6790 kilometres.
It has a maximum temperature of $-22°C$.
There is no life on Mars.

Task 1

Label the diagram.

Snakes

DIAGRAM

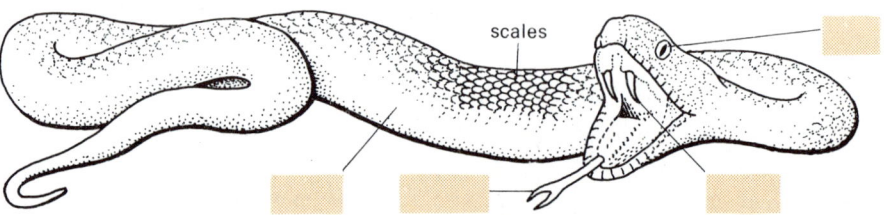

8

SUMMARY

SYSTEM	CHARACTERISTICS	
	body	
	tongue	thin
	teeth	
	limbs	

STATEMENTS
Snakes are reptiles.
They have a cylindrical body.
The scales on their body are smooth.
Their eyes are small and circular.
They have a thin tongue.
Their teeth are pointed.
They have no limbs.

Task 2   Label the diagram.

Task 3   Complete the summary.

Part 2
Language study

Patterns 1

Its diameter is 6790 kilometres.
= It has a diameter of 6790 kilometres.

Its maximum temperature is −22°C.
= It has a maximum temperature of −22°C.

Task 4   Use information in the table to complete the statements.

PLANET	DIAMETER (KILOMETRES)	MAXIMUM TEMPERATURE
Venus	12391	400°C
Neptune	50210	−220°C
Jupiter	142745	−130°C

9

1   ...... has a ...... of 50 210 kilometres.
2   ...... of 142 745 kilometres.
3   The diameter of Venus is ......
4   ...... is 50 210 kilometres.
5   The ...... of ...... is −220°C.
6   ...... has a ...... of 400°C.
7   Neptune ...... maximum temperature ......
8   ...... is −130°C.

Task 5   Use information in the table to complete the statements.

ELEMENT	ATOMIC NUMBER	ATOMIC WEIGHT	MELTING POINT	BOILING POINT
Sodium	11	22·9898	97·5°C	
Boron	5	10·81	2300°C	2550°C
Iodine	53	126·90	114°C	184°C

1   ...... has an atomic number of 11.
2   The ...... of ...... is 53.
3   Boron ...... 10·81.
4   The ...... of ...... is 97·5°C.
5   ...... has a ...... of 184°C.

Task 6   Correct these statements.
1   The diameter of Venus is 50 210 kilometres.
2   Jupiter has a maximum temperature of 142 745 kilometres.
3   Sodium has an atomic weight of 11.
4   Boron has a boiling point of 2300°C.

Patterns 2   *The length of the Nile is 6690 kilometres.*
= The Nile has a length of 6690 kilometres.
= The Nile is 6690 kilometres long.

Task 7 Use information in the table to complete the statements.

	LENGTH	WIDTH	HEIGHT	DEPTH
The Nile	6690 km			
The Straits of Gibraltar		20 km		
The St. Gothard Tunnel	14 km			
Vesuvius			1277 m	
The Newton Crater on the moon				14 000 ft
The Pacific Ocean				maximum 36 198 ft
Fujiyama			4132 m	
The Amazon	6900 km			

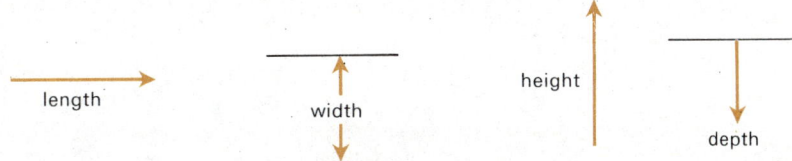

1 The St. Gothard tunnel . . . . . . length of . . . . . .
2 . . . . . . is 20 km.
3 The Pacific Ocean . . . . . . 36 198 ft.
4 The . . . . . . of Fujiyama is . . . . . .
5 The Amazon is 6900 km . . . . . .
6 The Straits of Gibraltar . . . . . . wide.
7 . . . . . . 1277 m high.
8 The Newton Crater . . . . . . deep

Task 8 Correct these statements.
1 The Amazon is 6900 km high.
2 Vesuvius is 1277 m long.
3 The Pacific Ocean has a width of 36 198 ft.
4 The St Gothard tunnel is 14 km deep.

Part 3
Discourse study   **Listing properties**

Task 9   **Selecting information**
Read the passage and complete table 1.

MARS
Mars is a terrestrial planet with two small satellites – Phobos and
Dermos. It has an equatorial diameter of 6790 kilometres. Temperatures
and pressures on Mars are low. It has a maximum temperature of about
−22°C and a minimum temperature of approximately −100°C. The
atmosphere is thin and consists mainly of carbon dioxide (95%). It has
permanent white caps of water ice and orange-red desert regions. There
is no evidence of life on Mars.

TABLE 1   CHARACTERISTICS OF MARS

type of system	terrestrial planet
temperatures and pressures	
maximum/minimum temperatures	
	thin 95% CO_2
colour	

Task 10   **Selecting and presenting information**
Use some of the information in table 2 to complete the passage.

Sodium is a soft . . . . . . with a . . . . . . density.   . . . . . . and . . . . . . points are
also low. It has an . . . . . . of 22·9898 and a . . . . . . of 0·971.

TABLE 2   PROPERTIES OF SODIUM (Na)

class	metal
texture	soft
colour	silver
density	low
atomic weight	22·9898
melting point . boiling point	low
atomic number	11
specific gravity	0·971

Enumerating properties

Task 11

Selecting information
Read the passage and complete table 3.

There are thirteen families of snakes. They all have a number of important characteristics. Firstly, their body is thin and cylindrical and has no separate tail. Secondly, the body is covered with hard, smooth scales. Thirdly, there are no external limbs.

Snakes have small circular eyes, a thin tongue and small pointed teeth.

TABLE 3:   IMPORTANT CHARACTERISTICS OF SNAKES

1	body with no	
2		scales
3		

Task 12

Presenting information
Use table 4 to complete the passage.

TABLE 4:   USEFUL PROPERTIES OF ALUMINIUM

1	light
2	ductile
3	malleable
4	good conductor of electricity

...... has several useful ...... Firstly, ... Secondly, ... Thirdly, ... extremely malleable. Fourthly, it is a ......

Part 4
Extension

Task 13

Read the passage and complete table 5.

artery   heart

blood

vein

capillaries

The human circulatory system consists of the heart, the blood vessels and blood.

Blood is a thick red fluid. There are about 6 pints of blood in the average human body.

There are three types of blood vessels: arteries, veins and capillaries. Arteries are large tubes. They carry blood to all parts of the body. Arterial blood is bright red and contains oxygen. Capillaries are tiny vessels. Veins are narrow tubes. They have thin walls and are inelastic.

The heart is a cone-shaped organ. It is located in the centre of the chest. It is a thick, muscular organ and has four chambers. The average heart is about 13 cm long, 9 cm wide and 6 cm thick. It weighs about 300 g.

TABLE 5

SYSTEM	PARTS
	1
	2 blood vessels
	3

14

Task 14   Now complete these tables.

TABLE 6

MEMBERS	CLASS
1	
2	
3 capillaries	

TABLE 7

TYPE OF BLOOD VESSEL	CHARACTERISTICS
1	
2	tiny vessels
3 veins	

TABLE 8

ORGAN	SIZE	SHAPE	NUMBER OF CHAMBERS	WEIGHT
the heart				

Unit 3   Structures (1)

**Part 1
Presentation**

The atmosphere

DIAGRAM

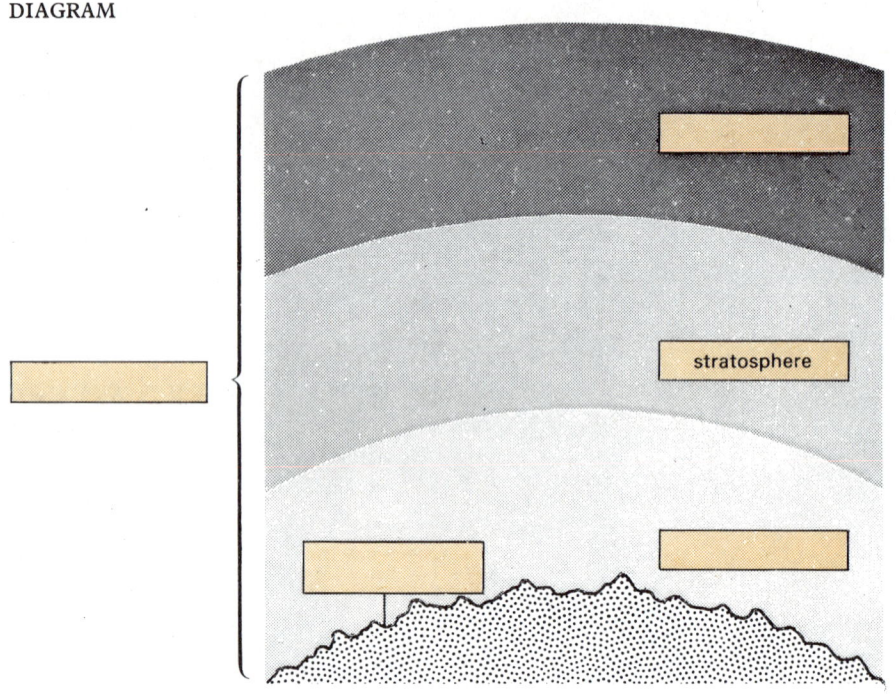

SUMMARY

SYSTEM	PARTS	LOCATION
the atmosphere	troposphere	above the Earth
	stratosphere	above the troposphere
	ionosphere	above the stratosphere

STATEMENTS

The atmosphere consists of three main parts.
The troposphere is next to the surface of the earth.
The stratosphere is above the troposphere.
The stratosphere is between the troposphere and the ionosphere.
The stratosphere is below the ionosphere.

Task 1

Label the diagram.

16

The ear

DIAGRAM

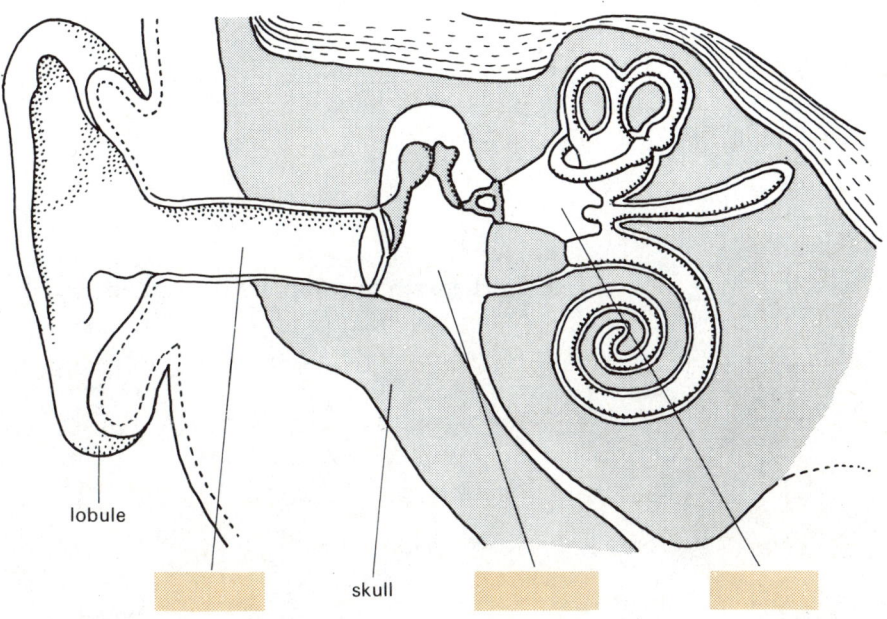

lobule

skull

SUMMARY

SYSTEM	MAIN PARTS	LOCATION
the ear		outside the skull
	inner ear	

STATEMENTS
The ear consists of four main parts.
The lobule is outside the skull.
The outer ear is located next to the lobule.
The middle ear is between the outer ear and the inner ear.

Task 2   Label the diagram.

Task 3   Complete the summary.

Part 2
Language study

Patterns 1	*The stratosphere is above the troposphere.* *The stratosphere is below the ionosphere.* *The lobule is outside the skull.* *The other parts are inside the skull.*

Task 4   Use the diagram to complete the statements.

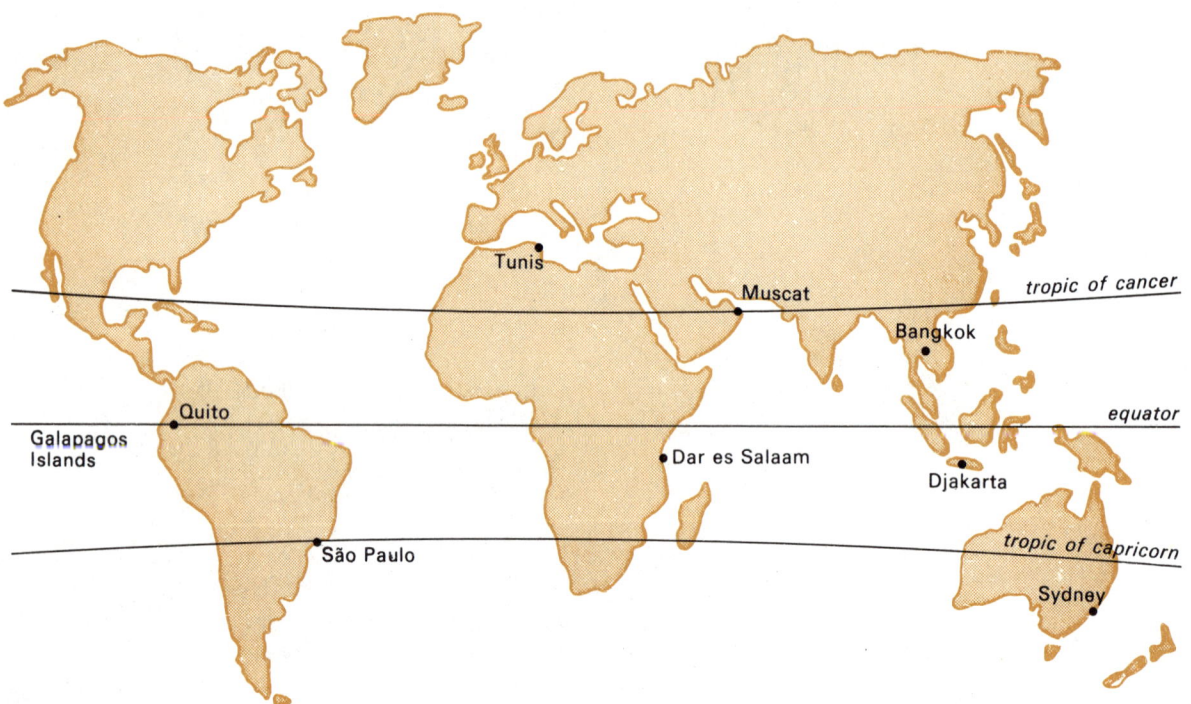

1   . . . . . . and . . . . . . are below the Equator.
2   Bangkok is below the . . . . . .
3   Sydney is . . . . . . the Tropic of Capricorn.
4   Bangkok is . . . . . . the Equator.
5   . . . . . . is above the Tropic of Cancer.
6   The Galapagos Islands and . . . . . . are on the Equator.
7   . . . . . . is on the Tropic of Cancer.
8   São Paulo . . . . . . the Tropic of Capricorn.

Task 5 Use the diagrams to complete the statements.

A CELL

A BERYLLIUM ATOM

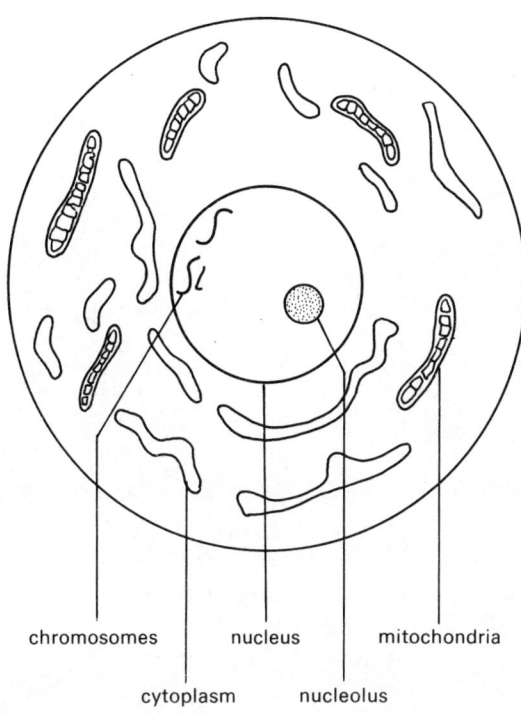

chromosomes   nucleus   mitochondria

cytoplasm   nucleolus

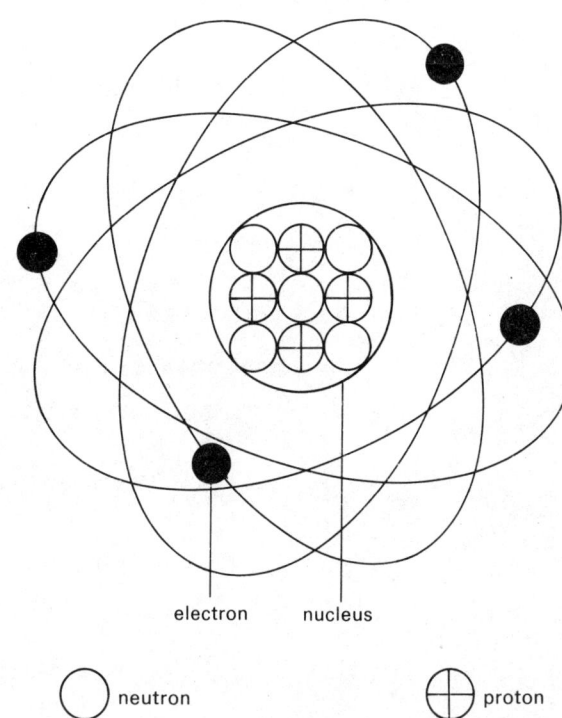

electron   nucleus

neutron   proton

1 The . . . . . . and the . . . . . . are inside the nucleus.
2 The mitochondria are . . . . . . the nucleus.
3 The cytoplasm is outside . . . . . .
4 The electrons are . . . . . . the nucleus.
5 The protons . . . . . .
6 The . . . . . . and the . . . . . . are inside . . . . . .

Task 6 Correct these statements.
1 Djakarta is above the Equator.
2 Quito is on the Tropic of Cancer.
3 São Paulo and Sydney are below the Tropic of Capricorn.
4 The chromosomes are inside the cytoplasm.
5 The protons and the electrons are inside the nucleus.
6 The nucleus is inside the neutrons.

Task 7   Use the diagrams to complete the statements.

THE EARTH

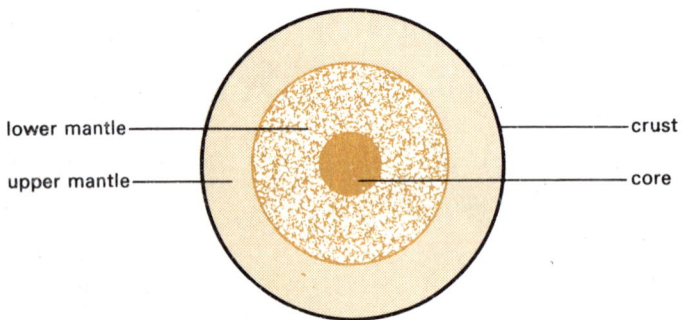

1   The lower mantle is between the . . . . . . and the core.
2   The . . . . . . extends from the lower mantle to the crust.
3   The upper mantle is between the . . . . . . and the . . . . . .
4   The . . . . . . extends . . . . . . the . . . . . . to the upper mantle.

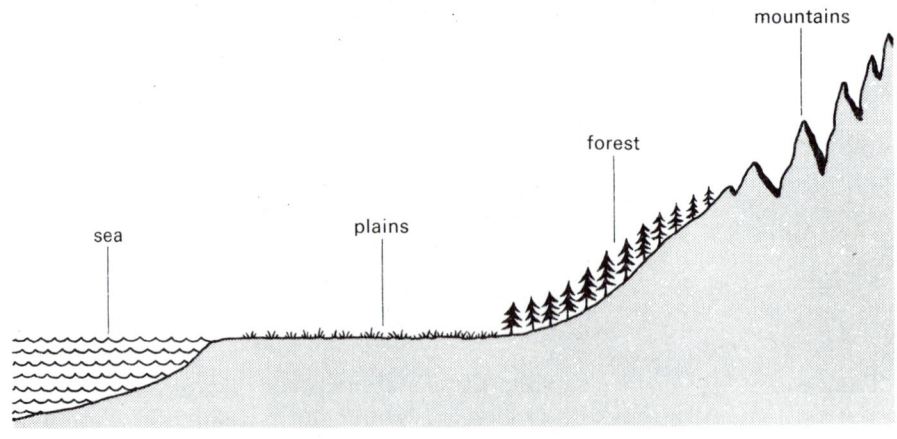

5   The forest is . . . . . . the . . . . . . and the mountains.
6   . . . . . . extend . . . . . . the sea to the . . . . . .
7   The forest extends . . . . . . to the . . . . . .
8   . . . . . . are . . . . . . the forest . . . . . .

Patterns 3   *The forest is located between the mountains and the plains.*
= The forest is situated between the mountains and the plains.

Task 8   Use the map to complete the statements.

A UNIVERSITY CAMPUS

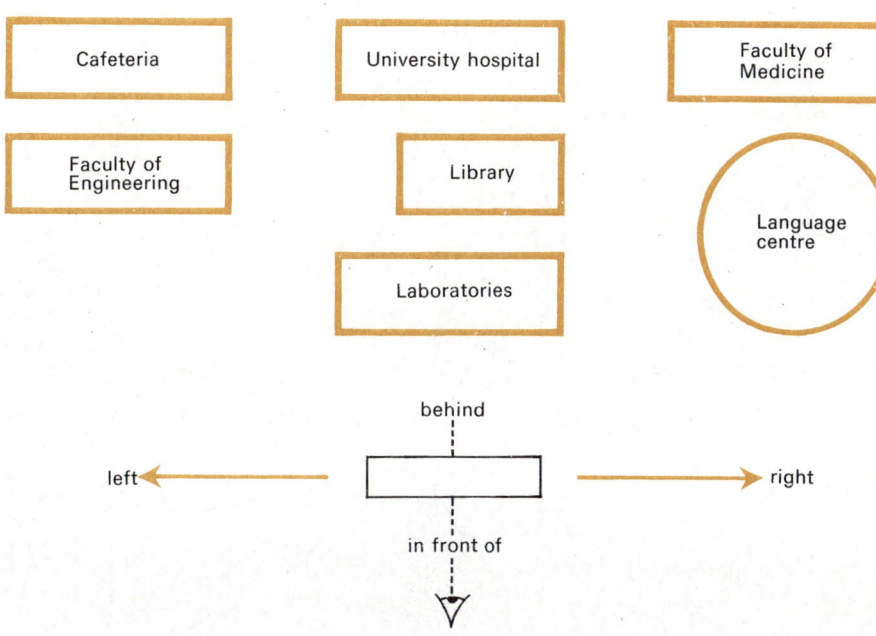

1   . . . . . . is located between the laboratories and the hospital.
2   The hospital . . . . . . between the . . . . . . and the . . . . . .
3   The Faculty of Medicine . . . . . . to the right of the hospital.
4   . . . . . . is situated to the left of the library.
5   The hospital . . . . . . behind the library.
6   The laboratories are . . . . . . in front of . . . . . .
7   The Faculty of Engineering . . . . . . the cafeteria.

Task 9   Correct these statements.
1   The cafeteria is situated in the centre of the campus.
2   The cafeteria is located to the left of the Faculty of Engineering.
3   The language centre is situated between the library and the laboratories.
4   The language centre is located to the left of the library.

21

Part 3
Discourse study

Spatial relations 1

Task 10

Selecting and organizing information
Read the passage and complete table 1.

THE EAR
Man has two ears. Each ear has four main parts:
1   **The lobule** is outside the skull.
2   **The outer ear** contains the eardrum, a thin membrane of skin.
Sound waves enter the ear and produce vibrations in the eardrum.
3   **The middle ear** is next to the outer ear. It contains three bones
which transmit sound waves to the inner ear.
4   **The inner ear** is next to the middle ear. It contains the cochlea.
Inside the cochlea is the corti, the organ of hearing.

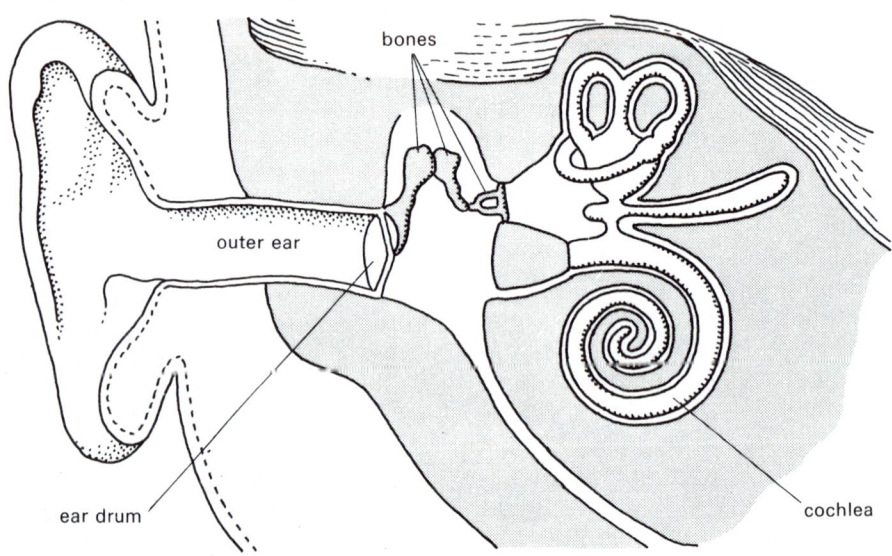

TABLE 1

SYSTEM	MAIN PARTS	OTHER PARTS	
Ear	1 lobule		
	2		
	3	three bones	
	4		

Task 11

Organizing information
Use the diagram to complete table 2.

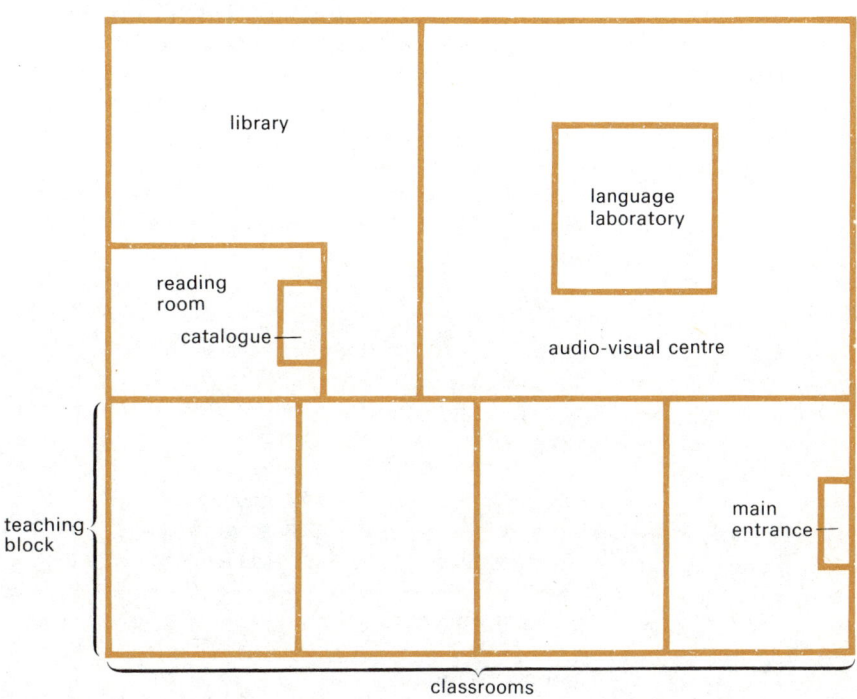

TABLE 2

SYSTEM	MAIN PARTS	OTHER PARTS	

Task 12

Presenting information
Use table 2 to complete this passage.

THE LANGUAGE CENTRE
The university language centre has . . . . . main parts.
1   The . . . . . . is next to the main entrance. It . . . . . . classrooms.
2   . . . . . . contains the language laboratory.
3   The library . . . . . .   Inside the . . . . . . is the . . . . . .

Spatial relations 2

Task 13

Selecting and organizing information
Read this passage and complete table 3.

The atmosphere is a region of gases surrounding the earth. It consists of 78% nitrogen and 21% oxygen. It is divided into three main parts.

The bottom part is called the troposphere. It is next to the surface of the earth. It extends from sea level to an altitude of 10 miles.

The middle region is called the stratosphere and extends to an altitude of 50 miles.

Above the stratosphere is the ionosphere. It extends to a height of 300 miles above the surface of the earth.

TABLE 3

REGION	LIMITS		
troposphere	sea level to		miles
stratosphere			to 50 miles
ionosphere	50 miles to		

Task 14

Presenting information
Use table 4 to complete the passage about the earth.

TABLE 4

REGION	LIMITS
crust	surface to 40 kilometres
upper mantle	40 kilometres to 700 kilometres
lower mantle	upper mantle to core
core	diameter = 6500 kilometres

The ...... is divided into ...... main parts. The outer part is called the ...... It extends from the ...... of the earth to a depth of

...... The upper mantle ...... a depth of ...... to ....
is between the upper mantle and the core.   ...... is the central part of
the earth. It has a ...... of ......

Part 4
Extension

Task 15

Read the passage and label the diagram.

The sun is a sphere of hot gases. It is nearly 150 million kilometres from earth. Solar energy is produced in the central core of the sun. The surface of the sun is called the photosphere. On the surface the temperature is about 6000°C. Below the surface the temperature is about 35 million degrees centigrade. Above the photosphere is a thin layer of gas known as the chromosphere. The chromosphere is only a few thousand miles thick. It is located between the photosphere and the corona. The corona, the outer atmosphere, extends millions of miles into space.

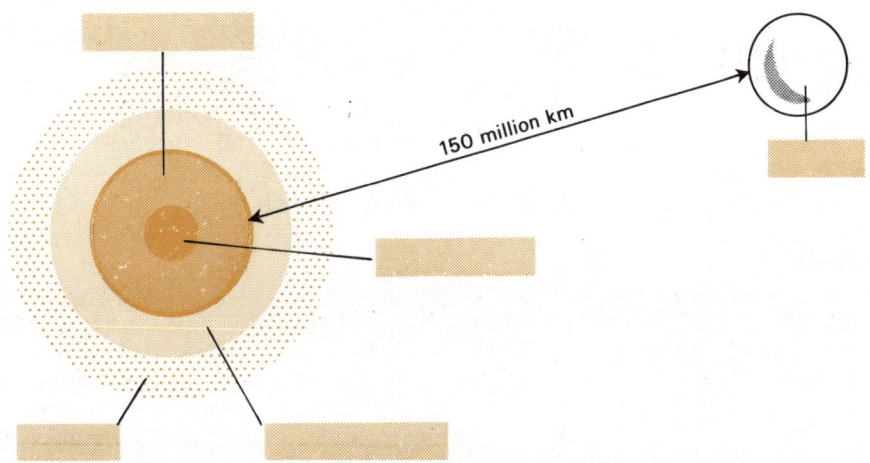

Task 16

Use information in the passage to complete these statements.
1   The earth is ...... kilometres from ......
2   The photosphere has a temperature of ......
3   The photosphere is ...... the chromosphere.
4   ...... is next to the surface of the sun.

Task 17

Answer these questions.
1   Where is solar energy produced?
2   Where is the temperature 35 million degrees centigrade?
3   Where is the corona located?

Unit 4   Structures (2)

Plants

DIAGRAM

SUMMARY

SYSTEM	CENTRAL PART	OTHER PARTS	RELATION TO CENTRAL PART
body of a plant	stem	flower	connected to the top
		leaves	connected to the sides
		roots	connected to the bottom

STATEMENTS
The body of a plant is composed of several parts.
The central part of the plant is the stem.
The roots are connected to the bottom of the stem.
The flower is connected to the top of the stem.
The leaves are attached to the sides of the stem.

Task 1   Label the diagram.

An electric torch

DIAGRAM

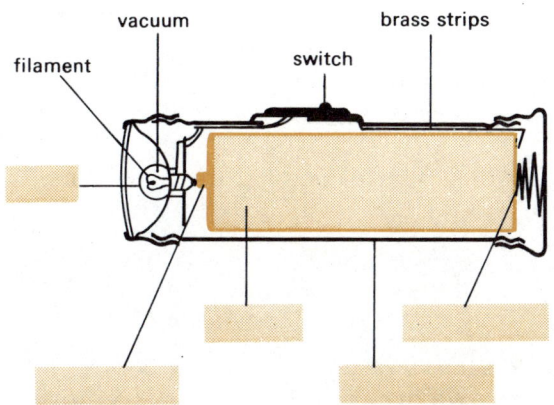

SUMMARY

SYSTEM	CENTRAL PART	OTHER PARTS	RELATION TO CENTRAL PART
			rests on the + terminal
			run . . . . . .
			encloses it

STATEMENTS

The central part of a torch is the battery.
The battery has two terminals.
The bulb rests on the positive terminal.
The metal case of the bulb is connected to the negative terminal.
Two brass strips run along the side of the battery.
The battery is enclosed in a plastic case.

Task 2   Label the diagram.

Task 3   Complete the summary.

Part 2
Language study

> **Patterns 1**
> *The flower is connected to the top of the stem.*
> *= The flower is attached to the top of the stem.*
> *= The flower is joined to the top of the stem.*

Task 4   Use the diagrams to complete the statements.

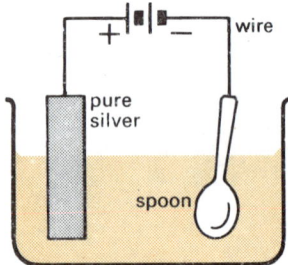

ELECTROPLATING: silver plating a spoon.
1   A piece of pure silver . . . . . . to the positive terminal of a battery.
2   A . . . . . . is attached to the spoon.
3   The spoon is connected to the . . . . . . of the battery.

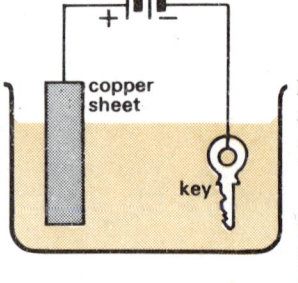

ELECTROPLATING: copper plating a key
4   A copper sheet is joined to the . . . . . .
5   . . . . . . to the negative terminal.

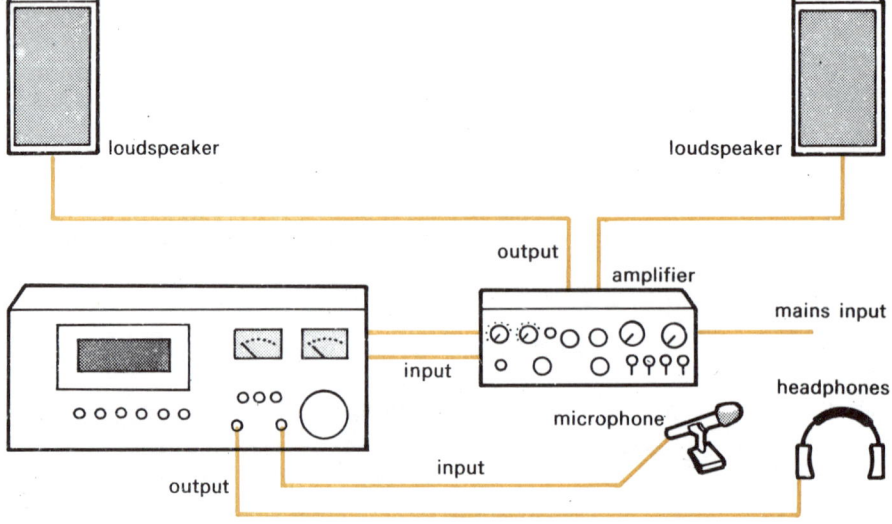

28

AN AUDIO SYSTEM

6 . . . . . . is connected to the tape recorder input.
7 The headphones are connected . . . . . .
8 The loudspeakers . . . . . .
9 The tape recorder . . . . . . the amplifier . . . . . .

Patterns 2

The strips pass along the side of the battery.
= The strips run along the side of the battery.

The strips run through the torch.
= The strips pass through the torch.

A strip runs from the switch to the battery.
= A strip passes from the switch to the battery.

Task 5

Use the diagrams to complete the passages.

THE CIRCULATORY SYSTEM

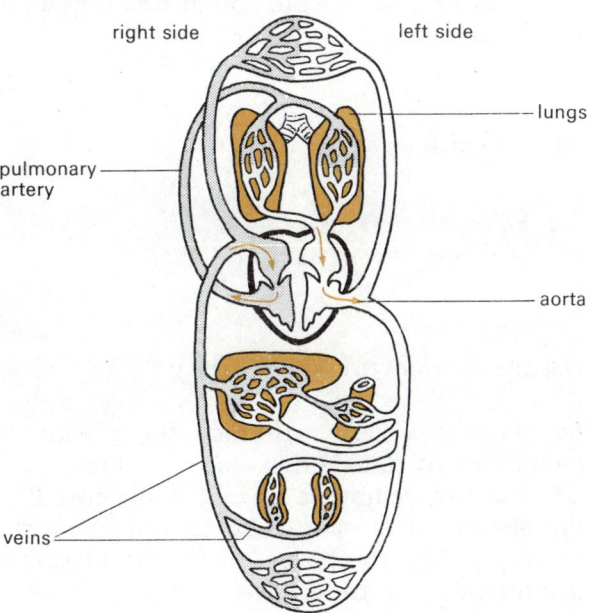

The blood leaves the left side of the heart and goes through the
. . . . . .   Then it goes through the whole body and returns in the . . . . . .
to the . . . . . . side of the . . . . . .   Then it passes through the . . . . . . into
the . . . . . .   It flows from the . . . . . . to the . . . . . . of the . . . . . .

29

THE AMAZON

The source of the Amazon is in Peru. The river passes through northern
...... It flows along the southern part of ...... It runs across
...... to the ...... Ocean. On its way it flows past ...... It reaches
the Ocean near ......

Patterns 3

The battery is enclosed in a plastic case.
= A plastic case encloses the battery.

The filament is surrounded by a vacuum.
= A vacuum surrounds the filament.

Task 6

Use the diagram to complete the passage.

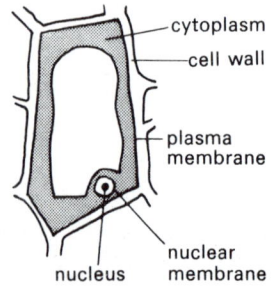

In plants a ...... surrounds the plasma membrane. The plasma
membrane surrounds the ...... The ...... the nuclear membrane.
The nuclear membrane ...... the nucleus. The ...... is surrounded by
the nuclear membrane. The nuclear membrane is surrounded by the
...... The cytoplasm ...... the plasma membrane. The plasma
membrane ...... the cell wall.

Task 7   Correct these statements where necessary.
1 The cell wall surrounds a plant.
2 A vacuum surrounds the torch switch.
3 The filament surrounds a vacuum.
4 The nucleus is surrounded by the nuclear membrane.
5 The plasma membrane is surrounded by the cytoplasm.

Part 3
Discourse structure   Describing the structure of a system

Task 8   **Selecting information**
Read this passage and label the diagram.

AN ELECTRIC TORCH
An electric torch is composed essentially of a bulb, a battery and a switch. The parts of the torch are enclosed in a plastic case.

The central part of a torch is the battery. The bottom of the bulb rests on the positive terminal of the battery. The zinc case of the battery forms the negative terminal. The negative terminal of the battery is connected to the switch by a brass strip. Another brass strip runs from the switch to the metal case of the bulb.

The bulb contains a very thin wire called a filament. The filament is made of a tungsten alloy and is enclosed in a vacuum. The filament rests on two glass columns. Two wires pass through the columns and the whole assembly is enclosed in a thin glass envelope.

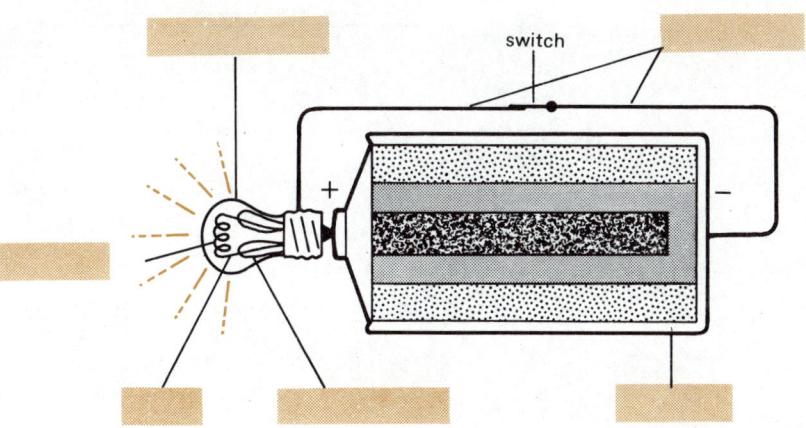

switch

+

−

Task 9   Complete table 1.

TABLE 1

PART	MATERIAL
torch case	
	zinc
strips	
bulb case	
	tungsten alloy
columns	

Task 10   **Presenting information**
Use the diagram and table 2 to complete the passage.

A DRY BATTERY

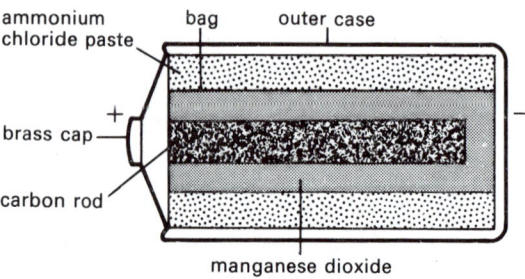

TABLE 2

PART	MATERIAL
outer case	zinc
cap	brass
rod	carbon
paste	ammonium chloride

The . . . . . . of a dry battery is made of zinc. On top of the . . . . . . there is a brass . . . . . . Under this cap . . . . . . rod. It is enclosed in a . . . . . . Inside the bag there is manganese dioxide. Between the bag and . . . . . . there is a . . . . . . of ammonium chloride. The whole assembly . . . . . . the zinc case. The outer case forms the negative terminal of the battery. The carbon rod and the . . . . . . terminal.

Comparing members of a system

Task 11

Selecting and organizing information
Read this passage and complete table 3.

PLANTS

All flowering plants are composed of four organs – roots, stems, leaves and flowers. The central part of the plant is the stem. The roots are attached to the bottom of the stem and usually grow underground. Some plants have one single root, others have many small roots. The leaves are connected to the sides of the stem. Some leaves are long and thin, others are fat and round. Some leaves are single, others are compound. The flower is attached to the top of the stem. Flowers contain the plant's reproductive organs. Most plants have the male and female organs in the same flower. Some plants have separate male and female flowers.

TABLE 3

ORGAN	DIFFERENCES	
roots	single root	
		fat, round
	simple	
	male and . . . . . . organs in the same	

Task 12   Use table 4 to complete the passage.

TABLE 4

PART	DIFFERENCES			
wings	2 pairs		none	
outer surface	thick		thin	
eye	compound		simple	
antennae	long		short	none

All ...... are composed of 3 parts – head, thorax and abdomen. Most insects have ...... of ...... attached to the thorax but some have no .... have a thick outer surface, ... outer surface. Most insects ...... eye ...... simple eyes.   ...... have ...... antennae, some have ...... and ...... have ...... antennae.

**Part 4
Extension**

Task 13   Read the passage and label the diagram.

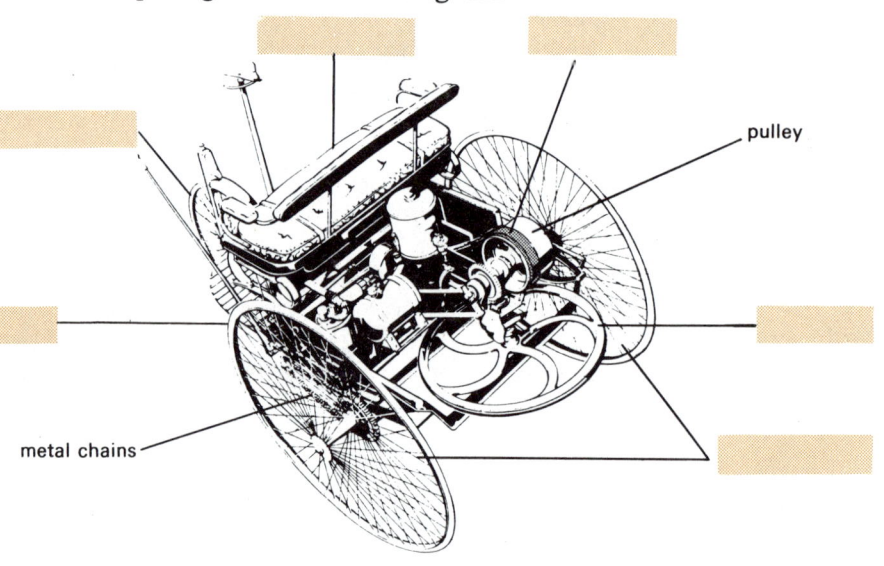

pulley

metal chains

AN EARLY MOTOR CAR (1885)

Benz's first car is now in a museum in Munich. It has one seat and three wheels. There is one small wheel at the front and two large wheels behind the driver's seat. The wheels are made of wood and are surrounded by solid rubber tyres. The chassis is very light and is made of steel tubes.

Between the two back wheels there is a heavy metal flywheel. To the right of the flywheel there is a pulley. A leather belt passes from the pulley to a shaft. The shaft is located under the driver's seat. Metal chains connect the shaft to the back wheels.

Task 14   Complete these tables. Use information from the passage in Task 13.

TABLE 5

PART	MATERIAL
chassis	
	wood
tyres	
flywheel	
	leather

TABLE 6

PART	LOCATION
the driver's seat	. . . . . . the large wheels
the flywheel	. . . . . . the back wheels
the flywheel	. . . . . . the pulley
the driver's seat	. . . . . . the shaft

Task 15   Complete these statements. Use table 6 to help you.

1 . . . . . . runs from the pulley to a shaft.
2 . . . . . . pass from the . . . . . . to the back wheels.
3 A leather belt connects the . . . . . . to the . . . . . .

Unit 5   Systems in action (1)

Part 1
Presentation

A computer system

DIAGRAM

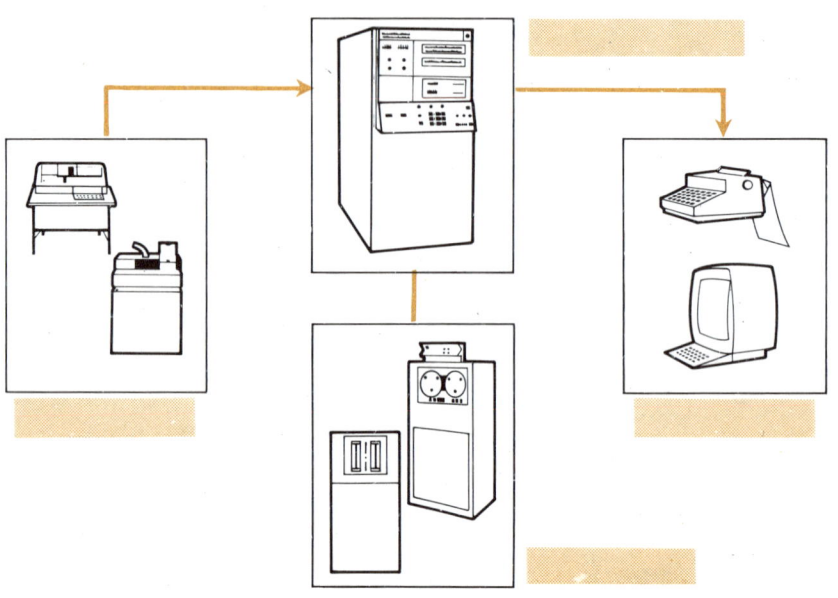

SUMMARY

PART	FUNCTION
input device	converts information into electronic pulses
central processor	performs calculations
memory unit	stores information and the programme
output device	presents information to the user

STATEMENTS
A computer system consists of a number of interconnected machines.
The input device converts information into electronic pulses.
The central processor performs the necessary calculations.
The memory unit stores the information and the programme.
The output device presents the information to the user.

Task 1

Label the diagram.

The motor car

DIAGRAM

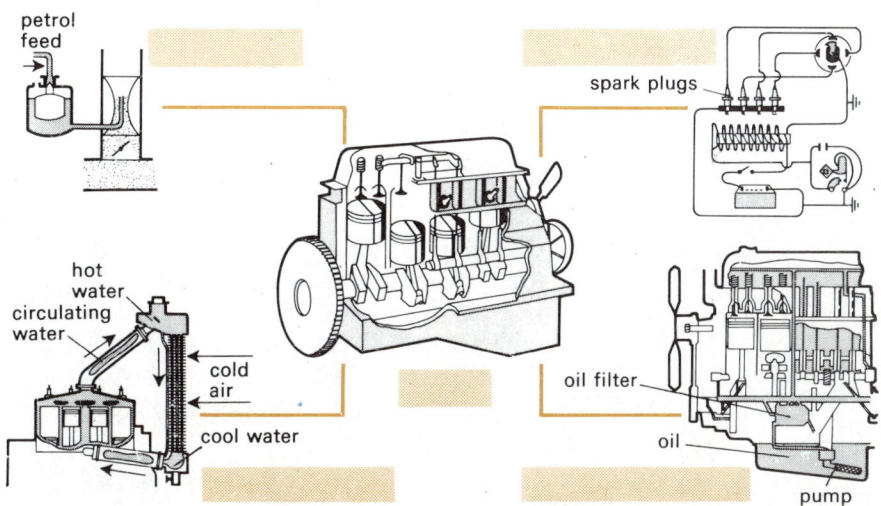

petrol
feed

spark plugs

hot
water
circulating
water

cold
air

cool water

oil filter

oil

pump

SUMMARY

SYSTEM	SUBSYSTEMS	FUNCTIONS
the motor car	engine	. . . . . . power
		supplies petrol
		. . . . . . spark
		. . . . . . excess heat

STATEMENTS

A motor car consists of a number of interacting systems.
The engine provides the power.
The fuel system supplies the engine with petrol.
The ignition system provides a spark.
The cooling system removes excess heat.
The lubrication system lubricates the engine.

Task 2   Label the diagram.

Task 3   Complete the summary.

37

Part 2
Language study

Patterns 1	The memory unit stores information.

Task 4

Match the parts of the body and their functions.

	PART		FUNCTION
1	the heart	a	break down food
2	the skeleton	b	carry blood
3	the kidneys	c	filter waste products
4	the hair	d	pump blood
5	the arteries	e	protect the body
6	the teeth	f	support the body

Task 5

Complete these statements.
1   ...... pumps blood through the body.
2   The arteries ...... from the heart through the body.
3   ...... break down food in the mouth.
4   The skeleton ...... and protects the internal organs.
5   ...... protects ...... from heat and cold.
6   ...... filter ...... from the blood.

Patterns 2	*The input device converts information into electronic pulses.*
	= The input device changes information into electronic pulses.
	= The input device transforms information into electronic pulses.

Task 6

Conversion of energy
Match the devices and the changes.

	DEVICE		CHANGE
1	a microphone	a	chemical energy→kinetic energy
2	a loudspeaker	b	kinetic energy→electrical energy
3	a steam engine	c	electrical energy→heat and light
4	a dynamo	d	electrical energy→sound
5	an electric light bulb	e	sound→electrical energy

Task 7

Write a statement about each device in Task 6.

Patterns 3   *The fuel system provides the engine with petrol.*
= The fuel system supplies the engine with petrol.
= The engine obtains petrol from the fuel system.
= The engine gets petrol from the fuel system.

Task 8   Match the foods and their nutrient content.

FOODS		CONTENT	
1	potatoes	a	fats
2	meat	b	carbohydrates
3	fruit	c	proteins
4	cereals	d	calcium
5	butter	e	vitamins
6	cheese		
7	green vegetables		

Task 9   Complete these statements.
1 Potatoes supply the body with . . . . . .
2 . . . . . . provides the body with fats.
3 Cheese . . . . . . with . . . . . .
4 . . . . . . proteins.
5 The body obtains fats from . . . . . .
6 The body . . . . . . from cereals.
7 . . . . . . gets calcium . . . . . .
8 The body . . . . . . carbohydrates . . . . . .

Task 10   Correct these statements where necessary.
1 Green vegetables provide the body with fats.
2 Fruit provides the body with vitamins.
3 The body obtains meat from proteins.
4 Cheese obtains calcium from the body.
5 The body obtains carbohydrates from potatoes.
6 Fats provide the body with butter.

Part 3
Discourse study

Lists of functions

Task 11

Read the passage and complete table 1.

A COMPUTER SYSTEM

A computer system is made up of a number of inter-connected systems. The heart of the computer is the central processor (c.p.). An input device converts information into electronic pulses and passes the programme and the data into the c.p.

The c.p. performs the necessary calculations and controls the input and output units. The c.p. is divided into 3 parts. The memory unit stores the data and the programme. The control unit selects data and instructions from the memory unit, interprets them and controls the calculations. The arithmetic unit adds, substracts and compares data.

The output device converts electronic pulses back into information and presents the information to the user.

TABLE 1

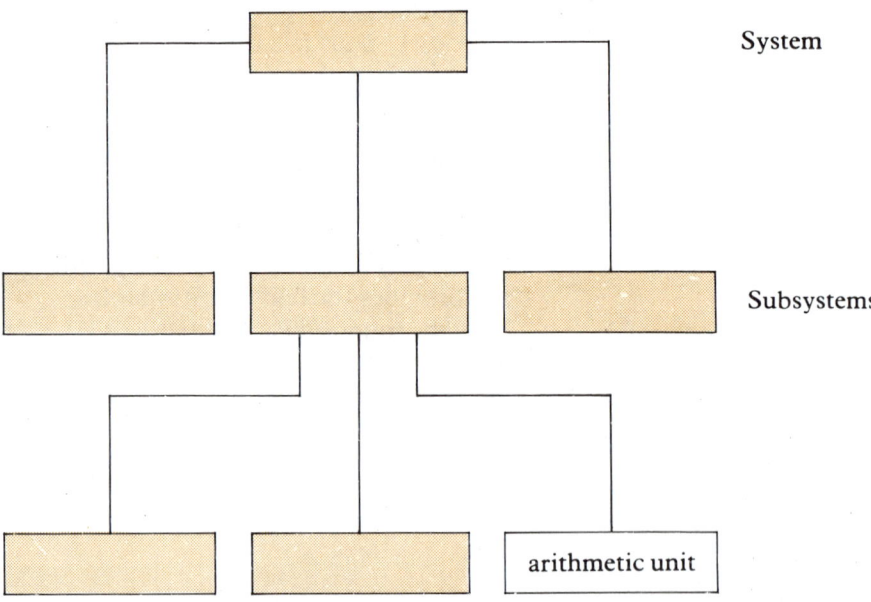

System

Subsystems

arithmetic unit

Task 12

Now read the passage on computer systems again and complete table 2.

TABLE 2

SUBSYSTEM/UNIT	FUNCTION
input device	1 converts information into electronic pulses 2
	1 performs calculations 2
memory unit	stores data and the programme
output device	1 2 presents information to the user

Task 13   Match the parts and their functions in table 3.

TABLE 3

PART	FUNCTION
1 leaves	a carry materials to the leaves b fix the plant in the soil
2 stems	c manufacture food substances d support the leaves
3 roots	e carry food from the leaves f absorb water

Task 14   Use table 3 to complete this passage.

The organs of a . . . . . . perform different functions.   . . . . . . manufacture food substances.   . . . . . . have several functions. Firstly, they carry materials from the . . . . . . to the leaves.   . . . . . .   Thirdly, they . . . . . to other parts of the plant.   . . . . . . fix the plant in the soil. They also . . . . . . and minerals.

Describing the behaviour of a system

Task 15   Read the passage and complete table 4.

THE MOTOR CAR
A motor car consists of a number of interacting systems.

The heart of the car is the engine. The engine provides the power to turn the car's wheels. The engine receives fuel from the fuel system.

The fuel is exploded in the cylinders. The explosion is produced by a spark. The spark is provided by the ignition system. Excess heat is removed from the engine by the cooling system. The moving parts of the engine are lubricated by the lubrication system.

TABLE 4

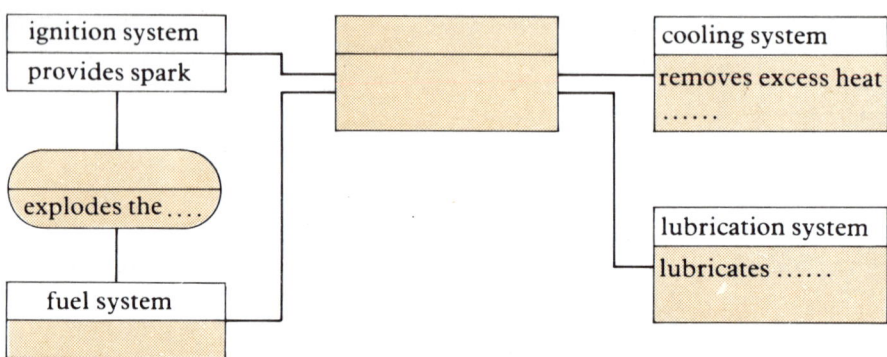

Task 16   Use the diagram to complete the passage.

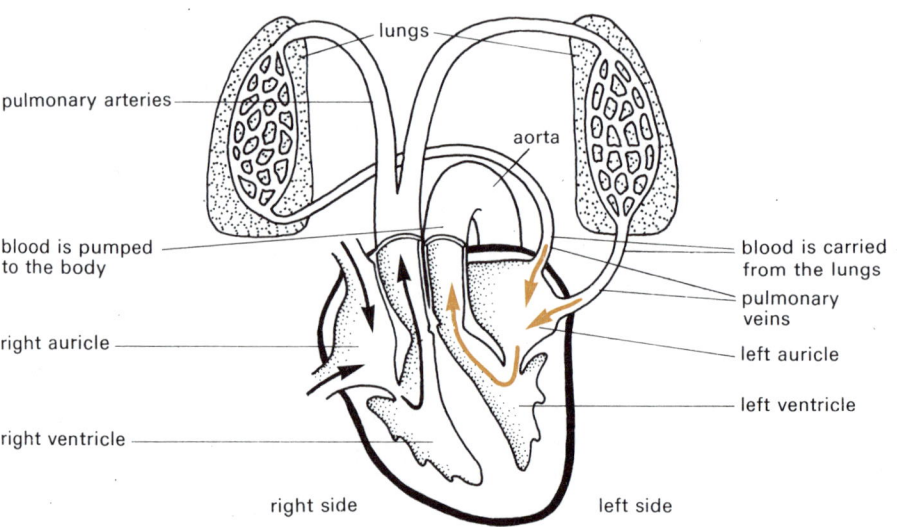

The pulmonary veins carry blood from the . . . . . . to the . . . . . .   The . . . . . . receives blood from the pulmonary veins. The left ventricle receives blood from the . . . . . . and . . . . . . it to the body. The aorta . . . . . . blood to the . . . . . .   The . . . . . . receives blood from the body and the right ventricle . . . . . . it to the . . . . . .

Part 4
Extension

Task 17

Read the passage and complete table 5.

BEE SOCIETIES
A bee society consists of a large number of sterile females (workers), some males and a queen.

The queen lives in the centre of the hive. She lays the eggs. The males fertilize the queen's eggs. The worker bees perform all the other activities of the colony.

The behaviour of the workers shows considerable division of labour. Some bees build the structure of the combs. Others inspect the development of the larvae. Some bees protect the entrance of the hive. A large number of bees collect pollen. Others make honey. They store the honey in the outer cells. The bee keeper collects the honey from the hive once a year.

TABLE 5

TYPE OF BEE	FUNCTION
queen	
	perform all other activities

Task 18

List the activities of the workers.

Unit 6 Systems in action (2)

Part 1
Presentation

Computers in space navigation

DIAGRAM

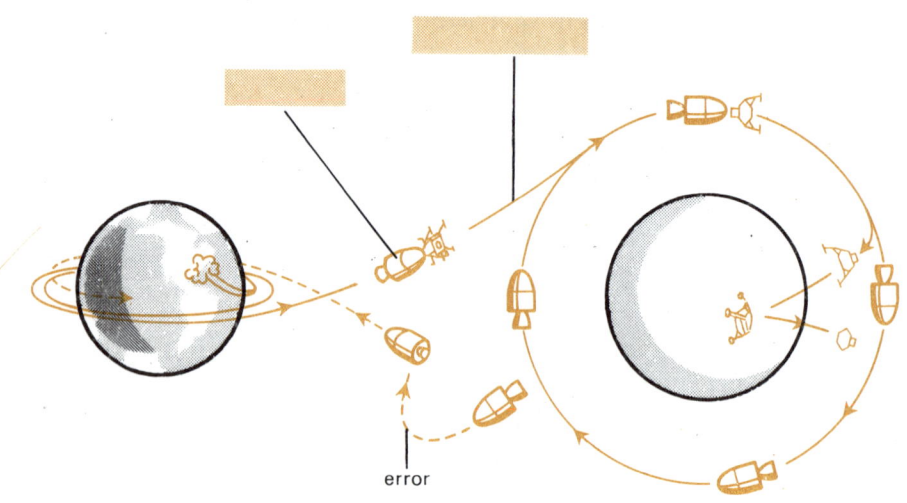

error

SUMMARY

NECESSITY	COMPUTER'S CAPABILITIES
Make complex calculations	Perform extremely complex calculations
Follow a precise path	Calculate the rocket's path
Correct errors	Correct errors

STATEMENTS
In space navigation it is necessary to make complex calculations.
A computer is able to perform extremely complex calculations.
A rocket has to follow a precise path.
A computer can calculate the rocket's path.
It is necessary to correct errors in the rocket's path.
A computer can correct errors in the rocket's path.

Task 1

Label the diagram.

Bats

DIAGRAM

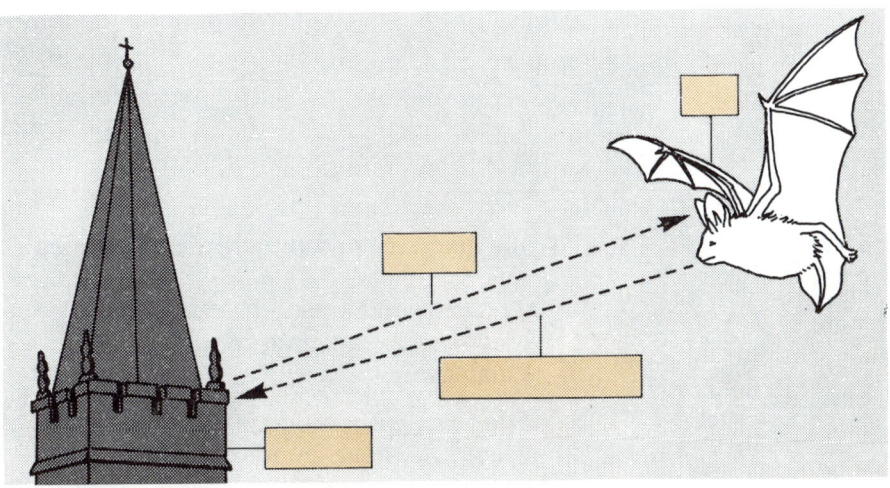

SUMMARY

NECESSITY	BAT'S CAPABILITIES
	1 emit . . . . . . 2 . . . . . . the echoes of . . . . . . 3 locate . . . . . . 4 . . . . . . objects in their path

STATEMENTS
Bats fly at night.
They cannot see well in the dark.
They have to avoid objects in their path.
A bat uses a type of radar system.
Bats emit ultra-sonic sounds.
They are able to hear the echoes of these sounds.
They are able to locate objects in their path.
They can avoid objects in their path.

Task 2   Label the diagram.

Task 3   Complete the summary.

Part 2
Language study

Patterns 1	*A computer can calculate the rocket's path.* *= A computer is able to calculate the rocket's path.* *A bat cannot see well in the dark.* *= A bat is not able to see well in the dark.*

Task 4

Use the diagrams to complete these statements.

ABILITY TO HEAR FREQUENCIES

1   A man can hear sounds of . . . . . . cycles.
2   A man cannot . . . . . . of . . . . . . cycles.

3   A dog . . . . . . hear sounds of 30 000 cycles.
4   Dogs . . . . . . hear sounds of 50 000 cycles.

5   Bats . . . . . . 120 000 cycles.
6   Bats . . . . . . 100 000 cycles.

7   Dolphins . . . . . . of up to . . . . . .

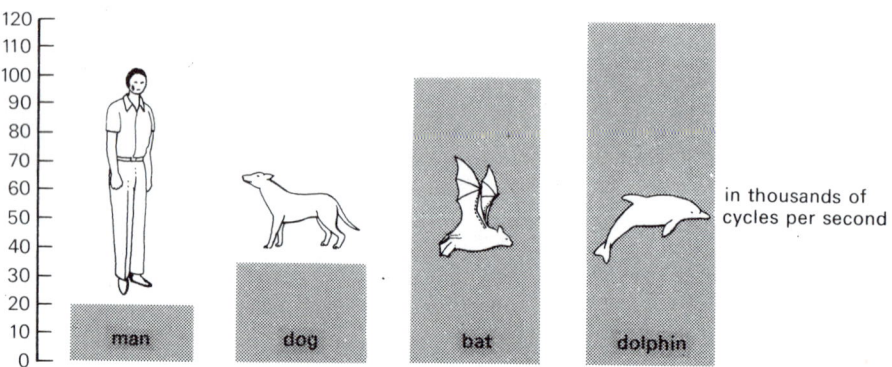

in thousands of
cycles per second

THE SPEED OF MAN AND ANIMALS OVER 100 YARDS

8   A man is able to run at speeds of up to . . . . . . miles an hour.
9   Men are not able to run at . . . . . . miles per hour.

10   Horses . . . . . . travel at a speed of 44 miles per hour.
11   Dogs . . . . . . at 44 miles per hour. They . . . . . . run at 40 miles per hour.
12   Antelopes . . . . . . move at speeds of over 50 miles per hour. They . . . . . . at 100 miles per hour.

46

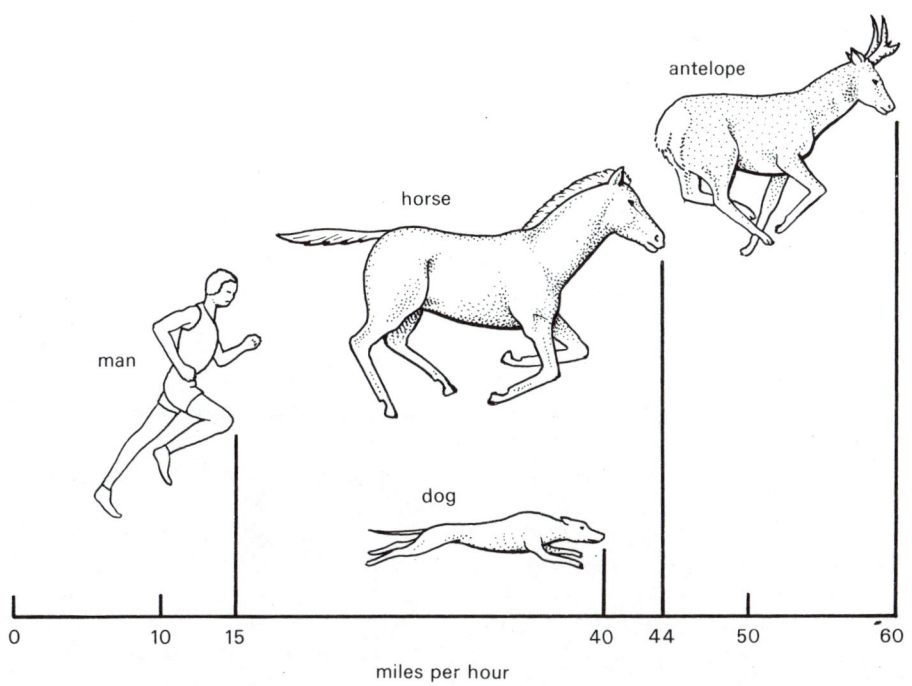

miles per hour

Patterns 2	*Bats have to avoid objects in their path.* *= Bats must avoid objects in their path.* *= It is necessary (for bats) to avoid objects in their path.*

Task 5   Use information in the list to complete the passage.

ACTIONS OF THE DIGESTIVE SYSTEM

> 1   obtain food from the environment
>
> 2   alter the chemical composition of food
>
> 3   pass food into the circulatory system
>
> 4   distribute food throughout the body
>
> 5   eliminate waste

Animals are not able to manufacture food substances in their bodies. They . . . . . . obtain . . . . . .   The body . . . . . . alter . . . . . .   It is . . . . . . pass food . . . . necessary . . . . . . throughout the body. The body is not able to use all the materials in food. It . . . . . . waste.

47

Patterns 3   *system ─────────────→ capability*
A bat uses a type of radar system. It can avoid objects.
= A bat's radar system enables it to avoid objects.

Task 6   Use the diagram to match the parts and the abilities.

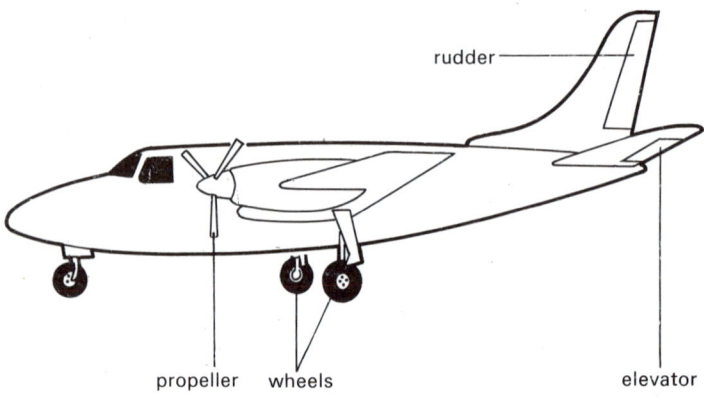

	PARTS		ABILITIES
1	the radio	a	the pilot knows the height of the plane
2	the wheels	b	the plane can move forward
3	the propellers	c	the aeroplane can land
4	the rudder	d	the pilot can communicate with the control tower
5	the elevator	e	the plane can turn
6	the altimeter	f	the plane can ascend or descend

Task 7   Write a statement for each part in the list in Task 6.

Task 8   Correct these statements where necessary.
1   Birds enable wings to fly.
2   The reproductive system enables animals to digest food.
3   Computers enable man to perform complex calculations.
4   Wings enable bats to fly.
5   A radar system enables bats to see in the dark.
6   Rockets enable computers to travel at the correct velocity.

48

Part 3
Discourse study   **Addition and equivalence**

Task 9   Read the passage and complete table 1.

COMPUTERS IN SPACE NAVIGATION
In space navigation it is necessary to make complex calculations. Computers are able to perform extremely complex calculations. A rocket has to follow a precise path. In other words it has to leave the earth's orbit at a precise moment. In addition, it has to enter the moon's orbit at a precise moment. A computer can perform the complex calculations which are necessary to work out the rocket's path precisely. Any errors in the rocket's path must be corrected immediately. A computer can control the rocket's progress. That is, it can both detect errors and correct them.

TABLE 1

NECESSITIES	COMPUTER'S CAPABILITIES
A rocket has to follow . . . . . . = 1 It has to leave 2	A computer is able to . . . . . .
Errors	A computer can . . . . . . = 1 it can . . . . . . errors 2 . . . . . .

Task 10   Use table 2 to complete the passage.

TABLE 2

VALUE OF WATER	USES
Water is necessary for life. = No living thing can exist without water.	1 animals: all the processes of the body 2 plants: growth 3 washing 4 producing electricity

Water is necessary for life. In other words . . . . . .   It is necessary for both plants and . . . . . .   Animals need water for . . . . cannot grow without . . . . . .   In addition, water is used for . . . . . . and . . . . . .

49

Contrast

Task 11   Read the passage and complete table 3.

BATS

The bat is the only mammal that flies. Unlike birds, which are generally diurnal, bats are nocturnal and fly at night. They have very good hearing but poor eyesight. They cannot see well in the dark. They can see objects which are very near them but they cannot see distant objects. They can see moving objects but not stationary ones.

In order to avoid objects in their path they use a type of radar system. They emit ultra-sonic sounds and are able to hear the echoes of these sounds. Their radar system enables them to know the position of objects in their path and to avoid objects at night.

They are able to fly at great speed but are unable to walk fast on the ground.

TABLE 3

WHAT BATS ARE ABLE TO DO	WHAT BATS ARE UNABLE TO DO
hear well	
see objects near them	
	see stationary objects

Task 12   Use table 4 to complete the passage.

TABLE 4

SUBSTANCE	SOLUBILITY IN WATER
Salt	√
Wood	×
Oil	×
Sugar	√
Sand	×

Water can dissolve many substances, but some . . . . . . do not dissolve in
. . . . . .   Water is able to dissolve . . . . . . but it cannot . . . .
is an insoluble substance . . . . . . is a soluble substance. Some substances
do not . . . . . . in water, but do dissolve in other liquids. Oil . . . . . . in
water but it does . . . . . . in turpentine.

**Part 4
Extension**

Task 13   Read the passage and complete table 5.

ADAPTATION
All living things must adapt to their environment. Some organisms are
able to look for suitable environments. Some organisms have to change in
order to suit their environment.

Some organisms are able to utilize food in their immediate surroundings.
Other organisms have to move in order to find food. A plant cannot move
but it can obtain food from its immediate surroundings. Its leaves and
roots enable it to obtain food from the atmosphere and the soil.

Birds travel long distances to obtain food. Their beaks are adapted to
catching insects, fish or other food.

A fish's respiratory organs are adapted to life in the water. It takes in
dissolved oxygen from the water. Its organs are not suitable for absorbing
oxygen from the air. The lungs of a man are adapted to breathing air.
They do not function in water.

TABLE 5

How do organisms adapt?	1 Some organisms look for . . . . . .
	2 Some . . . . . .
How do organisms obtain food?	1 Some obtain . . . . . . from their . . . . . .
	2 Other . . . . . .

51

Task 14   Now complete tables 6 and 7.

TABLE 6

	PARTS	FUNCTION	HOW THEY OBTAIN FOOD
Plants	leaves	enable plants to	
Birds		enable . . . . . . to	travel long distances

TABLE 7

	PARTS	FUNCTION	SUITABLE ENVIRONMENT	UNSUITABLE ENVIRONMENT
Man		enable man to	air	
Fish	respiratory organs	enable fish to . . . . . . oxygen		

Unit 7   Processes

Part 1
Presentation

The life history of a plant

DIAGRAM

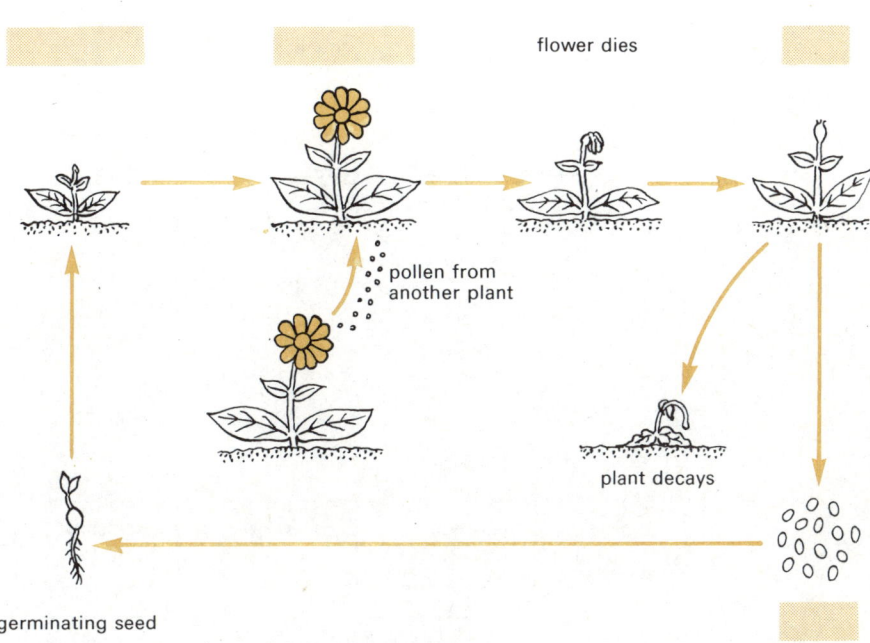

flower dies

pollen from
another plant

plant decays

germinating seed

SUMMARY	
Stage 1	Germination
Stage 2	Growth of the young plant
Stage 3	Maturity
Stage 4	Pollination
Stage 5	Formation of fruits
Stage 6	Decay of the plant
Stage 7	Germination of new seeds

STATEMENTS

A seed germinates in warm damp soil.
A young plant grows out of the seed.
The plant matures and flowers are formed.
The flowers are pollinated and fruits are formed.
When the flowers die the fruits remain.
The plant decays.
The seeds from the fruits grow into new plants.

Task 1   Label the diagram.

The thermostat

DIAGRAM

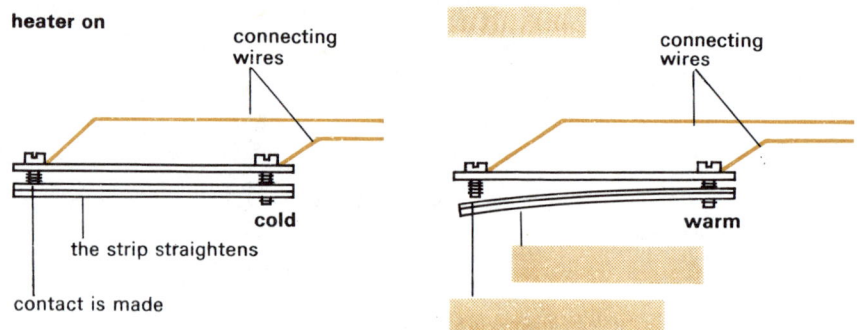

heater on

connecting
wires

connecting
wires

cold

warm

the strip straightens

contact is made

SUMMARY

A THERMOSTAT

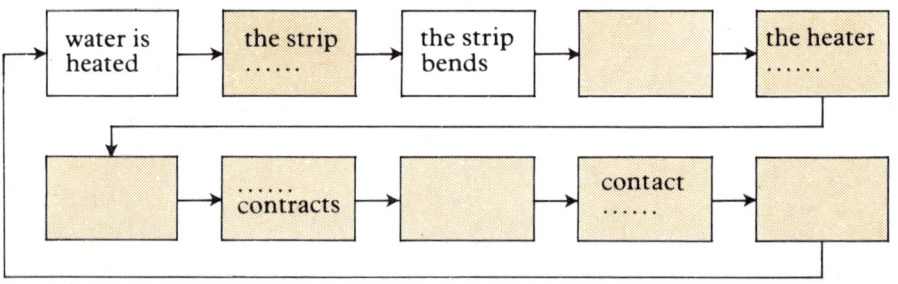

| water is heated | the strip ...... | the strip bends | | the heater ...... |
| ...... contracts | | contact ...... | |

STATEMENTS

The thermostat is connected to a heater in a hot water tank. The water in the tank is heated. The strip expands and bends. Contact is broken. The heater will be switched off. When the water cools, the strip contracts. The strip straightens. When contact is made, the heater is switched on again. The thermostat regulates the temperature of the water.

Task 2   Label the diagram.

Task 3   Complete the summary.

54

Part 2
Language study

Patterns 1   *The thermostat regulates the temperature.*
                       = The temperature is regulated by the thermostat.
                       = The temperature is regulated by means of the thermostat.

Task 4   Match each device and its function.

	DEVICE		FUNCTION
1	a thermostat	a	increases the strength of a signal
2	a hygrometer	b	moves fluids
3	a pump	c	measures humidity
4	a transformer	d	maintains a constant temperature
5	an amplifier	e	changes voltages
6	a dynamo	f	converts mechanical energy into electrical energy

Task 5   Complete these statements.
1   A thermostat . . . . . .
2   Fluids are moved by . . . . . .
3   Voltages are . . . . . . by . . . . . .
4   Mechanical energy . . . . . . into . . . . . . by . . . . . .
5   Humidity . . . . . . by means of a . . . . . .
6   . . . . . . the strength of a signal.

Task 6   Correct these statements where necessary.
1   Pumps measure humidity.
2   Amplifiers increase the strength of signals.
3   Voltages change transformers.
4   A thermostat is maintained by a constant temperature.
5   The strength of a signal is increased by a dynamo.
6   The cooling system removes heat.

55

Patterns 2   *When contact is made, the heater is switched on.*

Task 7   Use the diagrams to match these actions to their corresponding stages.

THE FOUR STROKE CYCLE

	STAGE		ACTION
1	Induction	a	The piston rises.
2	Compression	b	The piston rises. The exhaust valve opens.
3	Ignition	c	The piston descends. The inlet valve
4	Exhaust		opens.
		d	The piston is forced down.

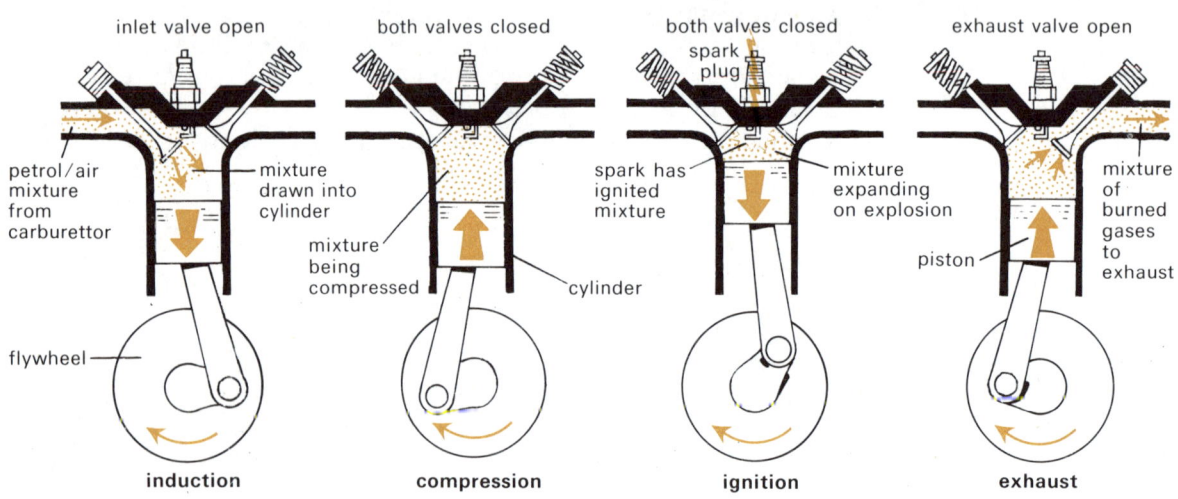

Task 8   Match the stages in Task 7 to these actions.
a   The gases are compressed.
b   A mixture of air and petrol vapour enters the cylinder.
c   Waste gases leave the cylinder.
d   The gases are ignited.

Task 9   Use your answers to Tasks 7 and 8 to complete these statements.

Induction	1	When the . . . . . . valve opens, ... enters the cylinder.
Compression	2	When the piston . . . . . ., the gases . . . . . .
Ignition	3	. . . . . ., the piston . . . . . .
Exhaust	4	. . . . . . the exhaust . . . . . ., ...

56

| **Patterns 3** | *When contact is broken, the heater will be switched off.* |

Task 10   Match the circumstances to their predicted consequences.

	CIRCUMSTANCE		PREDICTED CONSEQUENCE
1	air is heated	a	it falls
2	a seed has no oxygen	b	it rises
3	air cools	c	it does not germinate
4	ice is heated	d	it liquefies
5	a liquid is cooled	e	it solidifies
6	a liquid is heated	f	it evaporates

Task 11   Write a statement about each of the circumstances and consequences.

Task 12   Correct these statements where necessary.
1   When a seed is placed in warm damp soil, it will germinate.
2   When the strip expands, it will bend.
3   When ice is heated, it will solidify.
4   When the exhaust valve opens, the gases will be ignited.
5   When air is heated, it will rise.
6   When a plant decays, flowers will be formed.
7   When the heater is switched on, the water will be cooled.

**Part 3
Discourse study**   **Temporal relations**

Task 13   Read the passage and complete the table.

THE LIFE HISTORY OF A PLANT
First, a seed germinates in warm damp soil. In germination, a root and a shoot grow out of the seed. At the same time, the remains of the seed decay. Then a young plant grows and leaves are formed. When the plant matures, flowers are formed. The flowers are pollinated by wind, insects or water and then fruits are formed. After that, the flowers die. The fruits remain and the seeds from these fruits grow into plants during the following season. Before that the old plant decays. Decaying plants enrich the soil with chemicals. These chemicals provide food for other plants.

57

Germination	1 . . . . . . grow 2
Growth of the young plant	
Maturity	
Pollination	. . . . . . pollinate the flowers
Formation of fruits	
Decay of the plant	
Germination of new seeds	

Task 14

Number these actions to show their correct order.

The air passes through the bronchi.
The nose filters dust from the air.
The air passes down the trachea.
The air enters the lungs.
Air enters the nose.

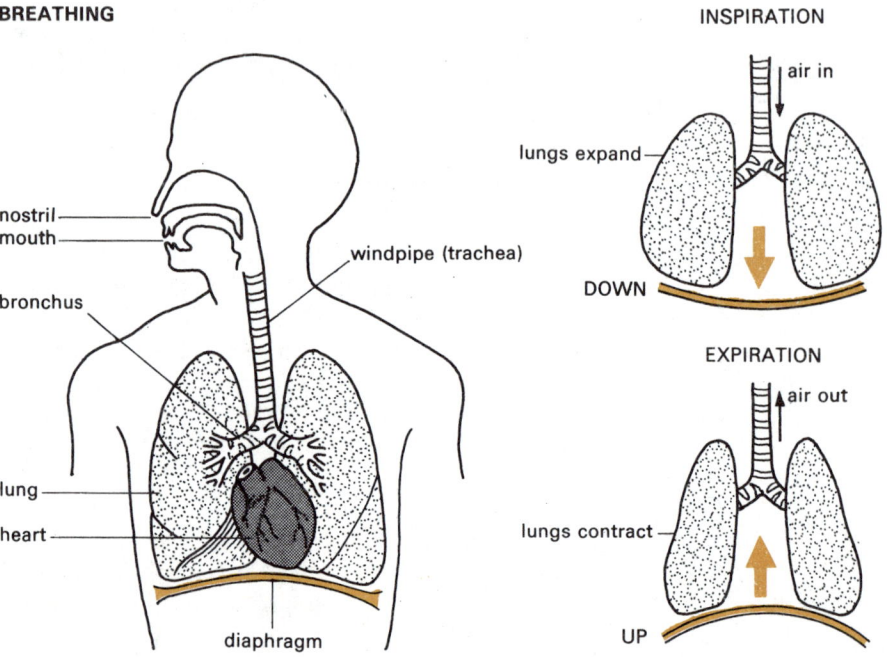

BREATHING

58

Task 15   Use the diagrams to match each action to its corresponding stage.

1   Inspiration   a   The diaphragm falls.
                   b   Air is forced in.
                   c   The lungs are compressed.
2   Expiration   d   The diaphragm rises.
                   e   Air is forced out.
                   f   The lungs expand.

Task 16   Use the information in Tasks 14 and 15 to complete this passage.

BREATHING
First the air enters ...... It passes through the nose. At the same time ...... Then the air ...... It passes ...... and ......
When the diaphragm ......, the lungs are ...... and air is ...... This stage is called ...... When ...... the lungs ...... and ...... This stage ......

Causal relations (1)

Task 17   Read the passage and identify the causes and the consequences in the lists below it.

THERMOSTATS
Thermostats are used in most water heaters. A thermostat consists of a bimetallic strip. It is connected to a heater in a hot water tank. The water in the tank is heated. Consequently, the strip expands and bends. As a result, contact is broken and the heater is switched off. After that, the water cools. Consequently, the strip will contract and straighten. As a result, contact is made and the heater is switched on again. In this way, the thermostat regulates the temperature of the water.

1   Water is heated.   The strip expands.
2   Contact is broken.   The strip bends.
3   Contact is broken.   The heater is switched off.
4   The water cools.   The heater is switched off.
5   The water cools.   The strip contracts.
6   The strip straightens.   Contact is made.
7   The heater is switched on.   Contact is made.

Task 18   Use the diagram to identify the causes and the consequences.

THE 2-STROKE CYCLE

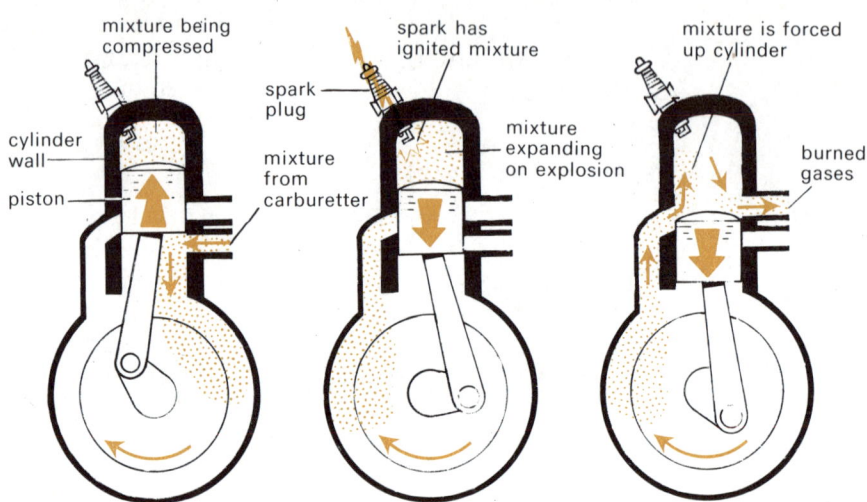

1   The petrol/air mixture en-   The piston rises.
    ters the cylinder.
2   The piston rises.   The petrol/air mixture is
                                 compressed.
3   The mixture is ignited.   A spark is produced.
4   The piston is forced down.   The mixture is ignited.
5   The piston goes down.   Exhaust gases leave the
                                 cylinder.
                                 The piston moves down.
6   The mixture is forced up
    the cylinder.

Task 19   Use your answers to Task 18 to complete this passage.

Some motor cycles use a 2-stroke cycle. This takes place in two stages.
First, ...   Consequently, the petrol/air mixture . . . . . . and is
. . . . . .   A spark is . . . . . ., and as a result . . . . . .   This forces . . . . . .
down. As a result, exhaust gases . . . . . . and . . . . . .

Part 4
Extension

Task 20   Read the passage and label the diagrams.

AN EXAMPLE OF BIOLOGICAL FEEDBACK : TAKING A GLASS OF WATER
The action of taking a glass of water requires a series of muscular actions. The memory contains a record of the necessary sequences. Consequently, the brain can send the necessary control signals through the nervous system. The control signals stimulate the arm muscles. As a result, the muscles move the arm in the necessary direction.

The hand approaches the glass. At the same time, the eye observes the progress of the hand. The eye sends information about the hand's progress to the brain. This information is compared with the memory's record of the action. Decision elements in the brain can send signals to correct any errors. Consequently, the muscular actions will change. These operations are repeated in many cycles. Finally, the glass is reached.

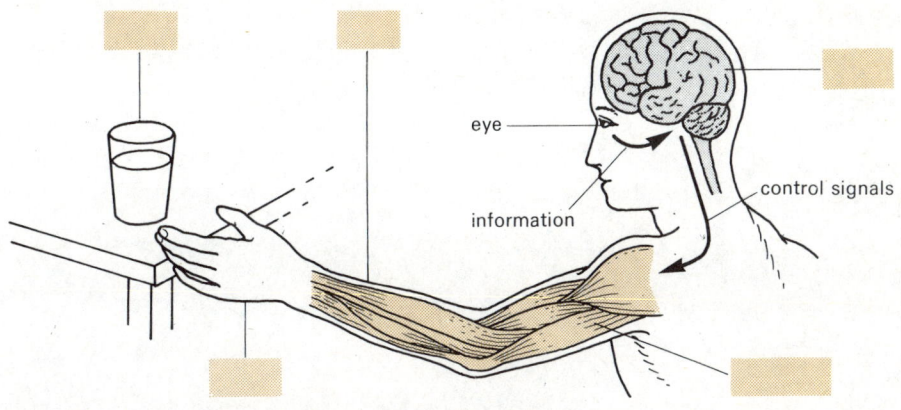

eye

information

control signals

Task 21   Complete these statements.

Stage 1 :   The brain sends . . . . . .
Stage 2 :   . . . . . . the arm muscles.
Stage 3 :   The arm . . . . . .
Stage 4 :   *i* The hand . . . . . .
            ii . . . . . . the hand.
Stage 5 :   The eye . . . . . .
Stage 6 :   The brain compares . . . . . . with . . . . . .
Stage 7 :   . . . . . . correction signals.
Stage 8 :   . . . . . .
Stage 9 :   . . . . . . reaches the glass.

Task 22   List the functions of the brain, the eye and the hand.

Task 23   Complete these statements:
1   The memory's record enables . . . . . . to . . . . . . the necessary control signals.
2   . . . . . . receives information about the hand's progress from . . . . . .
3   When . . . . . . occur, the brain . . . . . . signals to correct them.
4   The arm muscles . . . . . . by control signals.

Unit 8   Interactions

Part 1
Presentation

The refrigerator

DIAGRAM

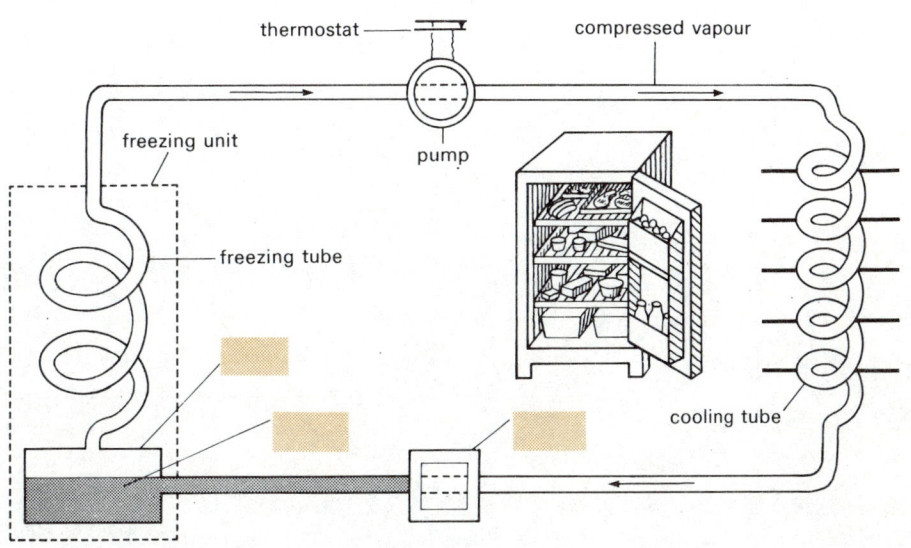

SUMMARY

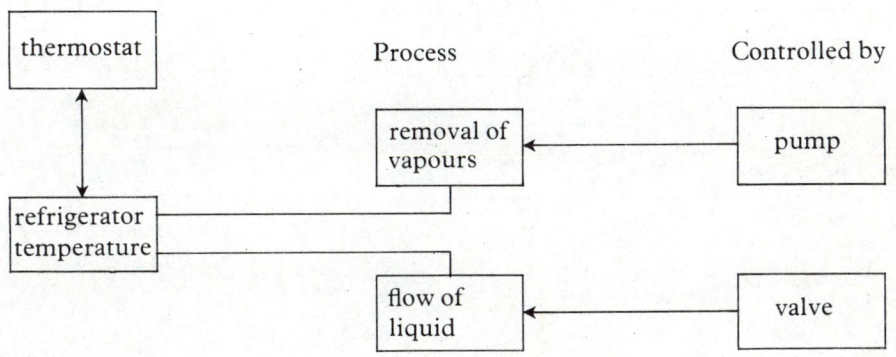

STATEMENTS

Refrigerators cool food.
The temperature of a refrigerator is controlled by a thermostat.
The thermostat is affected by changes in temperature.
The liquid in a tank evaporates.
The vapours are removed by a pump.
The vapour condenses. The liquid flows back into the evaporator.
The flow of the liquid is controlled by a valve.

Task 1   Label the diagram.

Soil

DIAGRAM

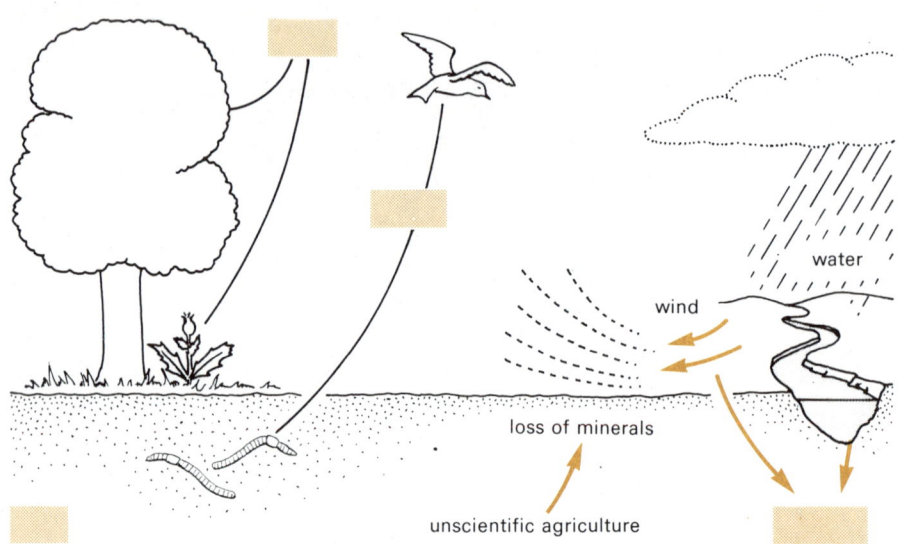

loss of minerals

unscientific agriculture

water

wind

SUMMARY

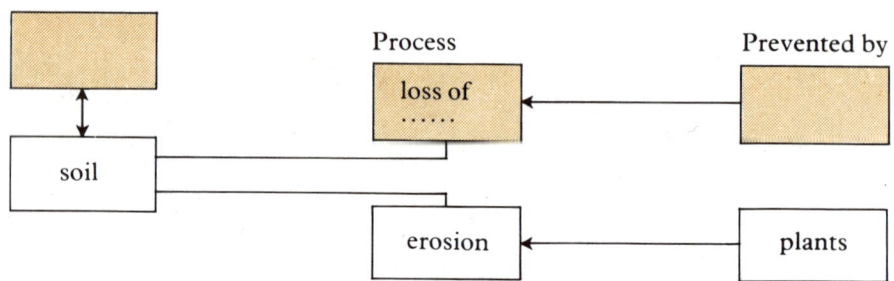

Process

Prevented by

loss of
......

soil

erosion

plants

STATEMENTS
Soil provides raw materials for plants.
The type of soil determines the flora and fauna of a region.
Soil is affected by the flora and fauna of a region.
Unscientific agriculture can cause soil to lose minerals.
Wind and water can cause erosion.
Fertilizers prevent the loss of minerals.
Some plants can prevent erosion.

Task 2   Label the diagram.

Task 3   Complete the summary.

Part 2
Language study

Patterns 1   *Unscientific agriculture can cause soil to lose minerals.*

Task 4   Match the causes and the effects.

CAUSE		EFFECT
	a	solids liquefy
1 heat	b	metals contract
	c	gases condense
	d	liquids solidify
2 cooling	e	liquids evaporate
	f	substances expand

Task 5   Write a statement about each cause and effect. For example, *Cooling causes liquids to solidify.*

Task 6   Correct these statements where necessary.
1   Heat causes liquids to solidify.
2   Heat causes liquids to evaporate.
3   Cooling causes solids to evaporate.
4   Fertilizers cause the soil to lose minerals.
5   Fertilizers cause the soil to gain minerals.
6   The expansion of the strip causes the thermostat to switch the heater on.

Patterns 2   *Plants prevent the wind from eroding soil.*
                     = Plants prevent erosion.

Task 7   Match the causes and effects.

CAUSE		EFFECT
1 lubricants	a	explosions do not occur
2 insulators	b	heat does not escape
3 gloves	c	heat does not damage engines
4 safety valves	d	hands are not injured
5 lightning conductors	e	lightning does not damage buildings
6 fuses	f	electrical equipment is not damaged

65

Task 8

Complete these statements.
1   Lubricants prevent . . . . . . from damaging . . . . . .
2   Insulators prevent . . . . . . from . . . . . .
3   . . . . . . prevent damage to electrical equipment.
4   . . . . . . damage to buildings.
5   . . . . . . prevent explosions.
6   . . . . . . injury to the hands.

Patterns 3

The liquid evaporates. The vapours are removed by a pump.
= *The liquid evaporates. At the same time, the vapours are removed by a pump.*
= *As the liquid evaporates, the vapours are removed by a pump.*

Task 9

Use this information to label the diagram.

water evaporates
the vapour rises
the vapour condenses
drops of water fall to the ground

RAIN

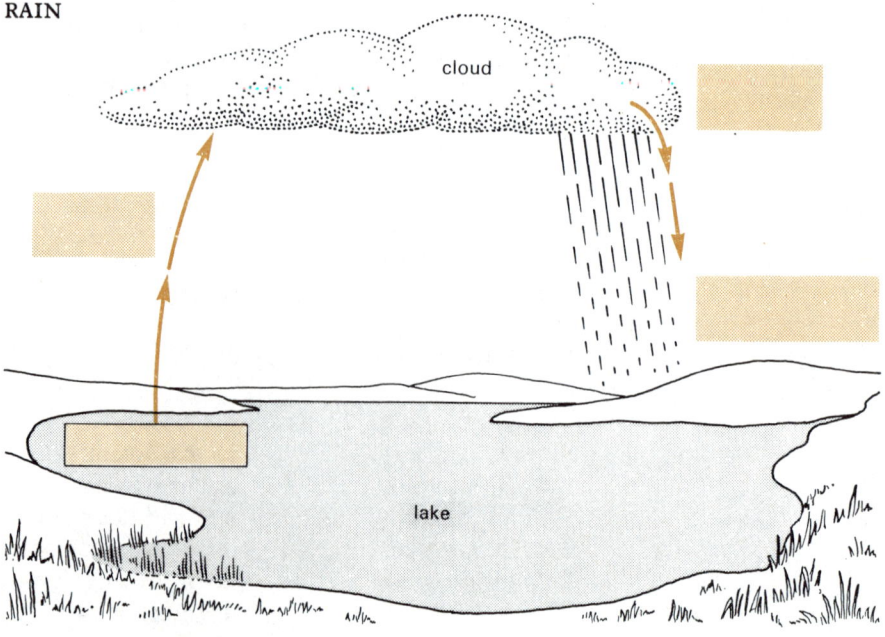

Task 10   Use this information to label the diagram.

the vapour becomes warm
the vapour is cooled
the temperature falls below $-40°C$
ice particles are formed
ice particles collide
ice particles increase in size and weight
ice particles fall
ice particles become warm
ice particles melt

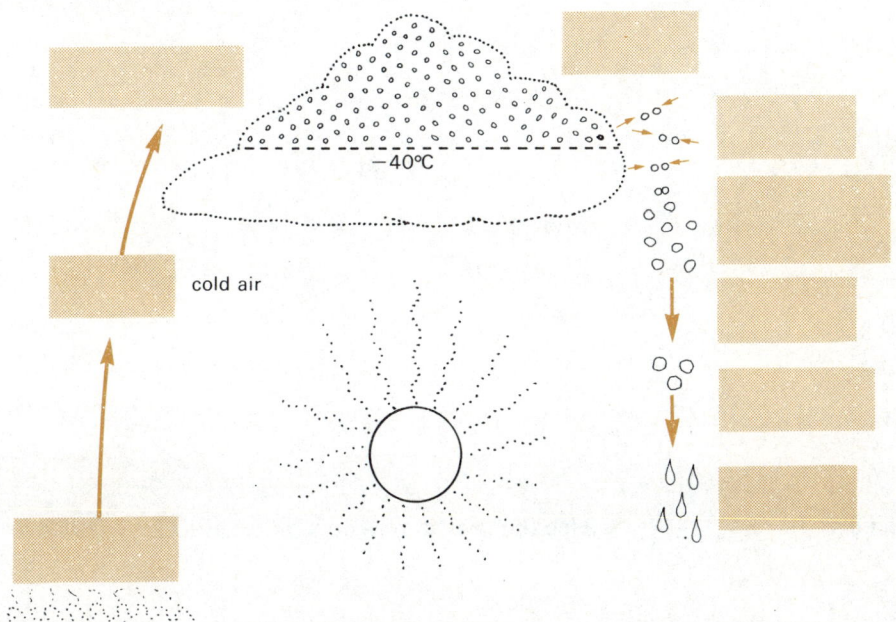

Task 11   Use the diagrams in Tasks 9 and 10 to complete these statements.
Water in rivers and oceans ......   As the vapour becomes ......, it
......   As it rises, the vapour ......   As the temperature ......,
......   As ......, they increase in size and weight. As they increase in
size and weight, ..., they become warm.   ......, they
melt. As the ice particles melt, ...

Task 12   Correct these statements.
1   As vapour is cooled, it rises.
2   As ice particles fall, they increase in size and weight.
3   As the temperature of ice decreases, it melts.

67

Part 3
Discourse study

Describing cycles

Task 13

Read this passage and complete table 1.

Refrigerators are used for cooling food. Cooling takes place when a liquid evaporates. As the vapours are formed, they are removed by a pump. Consequently the vapour is under reduced pressure and will evaporate rapidly. The vapour is pumped into a condenser. It is compressed and consequently turns back into liquid form. The liquid is passed back into the evaporator. The flow of the liquid is controlled by a valve. In this way, there is a continuous circulation of liquid and vapour.

The pump motor is controlled by a thermostat. The thermostat is affected by changes in temperature. When the correct temperature is reached, the thermostat switches the pump off. Rising warm air causes the thermostat to switch the pump on again. In this way, the thermostat regulates the temperature of the refrigerator.

TABLE 1

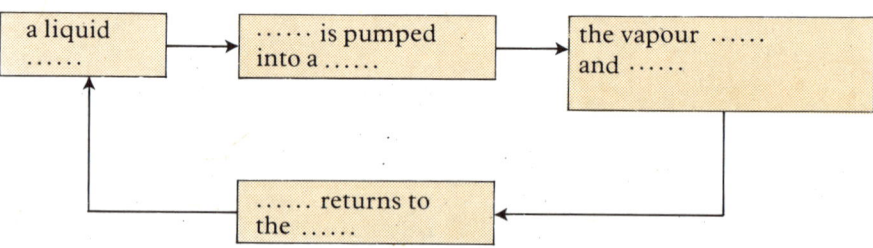

Task 14

Use the diagram to complete table 2.

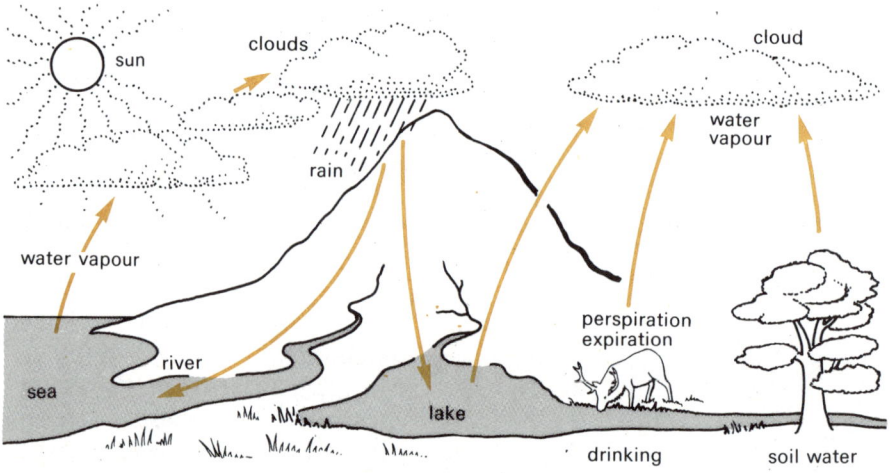

TABLE 2

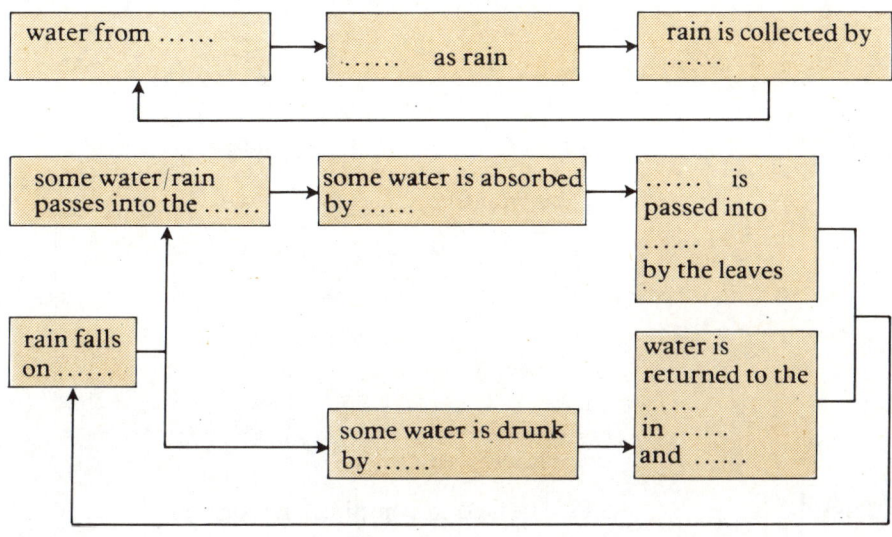

Task 15

Use table 2 to complete this description of the water cycle.

Heat from the sun causes ...... in ...... and rivers to .... as rain. Some of the rain ......   Some rain ...... the soil. This water is then ...... by the roots of plants and ...... by the leaves. Some water ...... by animals. The animals then ...... and ......   In this way there is a continuous cycle of ......

Causal relations (2)

Task 16

Read the passage and complete table 3.

Soil is an invaluable natural resource. It provides raw materials for the plants on which we depend for food. The soil and the living organisms of a region are inter-dependent. On the one hand, soil is affected by the flora and fauna of the region. On the other hand, the type of soil determines the flora and fauna of the region.

Consequently, damage to soil will destroy the balance of nature. It is a danger to human life and to man's economic security. Causes of damage can be physical or chemical. Damage can be caused by man or by natural phenomena.

Unscientific agriculture can cause a loss of minerals. Erosion can be

69

caused by wind or by flowing or falling water. There are several ways of preventing damage to soil, including the use of fertilizers to prevent loss of minerals and the use of grass and other plants to prevent erosion.

TABLE 3

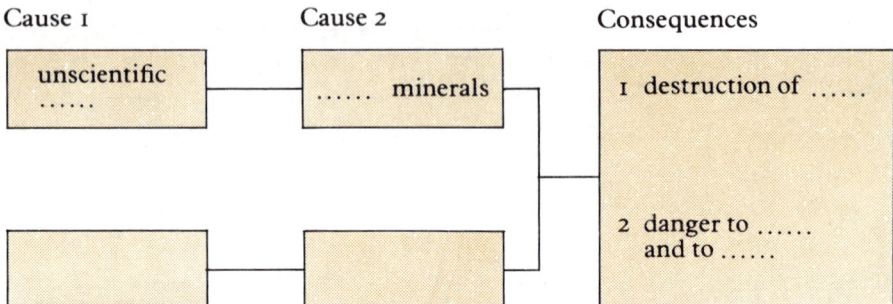

Cause 1	Cause 2	Consequences
unscientific	...... minerals	1 destruction of ......
		2 danger to ...... and to ......

Task 17

Use table 4 to complete this passage.

TABLE 4   POLLUTION

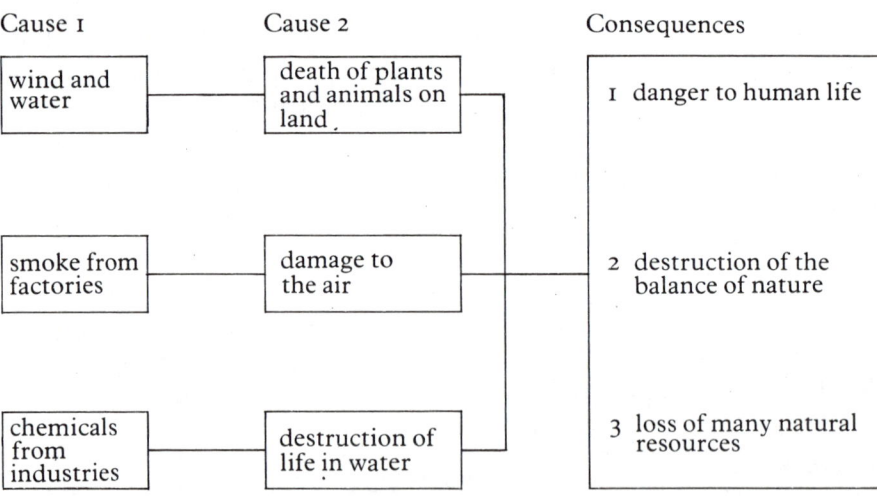

Cause 1	Cause 2	Consequences
wind and water	death of plants and animals on land	1 danger to human life
smoke from factories	damage to the air	2 destruction of the balance of nature
chemicals from industries	destruction of life in water	3 loss of many natural resources

Plants and animals depend on their ......   On the other hand, the environment ...... by the living organisms in it. Consequently, ... of the environment is a danger to ......   Pollution ...... the balance of nature and causes man to ......

Pollution can be caused by man or by .... can kill many ...... on land.   ...... causes ...... to the air.   ......from ...... life in ......

70

Part 4
Extension

Task 18   Read the passage and complete the table.

Plants and animals interact with each other. Animals depend on plants for their food. In the same way, plants depend on animals. All plants and animals must have four elements: carbon, nitrogen, hydrogen and oxygen. These elements are combined to form proteins, fats and carbohydrates in the animal or plant. They are then used for building cells and tissues or as a source of energy. Oxygen is obtained from air and water. Water is also a source of hydrogen for living things. Carbon and nitrogen come from the air, sea or soil.

The use of these four elements by plants and animals involves complex cycles. The cycles demonstrate the dependence of animals and plants on each other.

In the nitrogen cycle nitrates are absorbed from the soil by plants. The nitrates are used to make proteins. Plants are eaten by animals. When plants and animals die, bacteria in the soil cause decomposition. As the dead plant or animal is decomposed, the tissues are converted to nitrates. In this way, the nitrates are returned to the soil.

SOURCE OF THE ELEMENTS	ELEMENT	WHAT THE ELEMENTS ARE USED FOR
	1	combined to form . . . . . .
water	2	. . . . . .
	3	or
	4	. . . . . .

Task 19   Draw a diagram based on this description of the nitrogen cycle.

Task 20   Complete these statements.
1   Living things obtain . . . . . . from water.
2   The air provides . . . . . .
3   Roots absorb . . . . . . from the . . . . . .
4   Bacteria cause . . . . . . to decompose.
5   . . . . . . depend on each other.

71

Unit 9   Evolution of systems

Part 1
Presentation

The earth before man

DIAGRAM

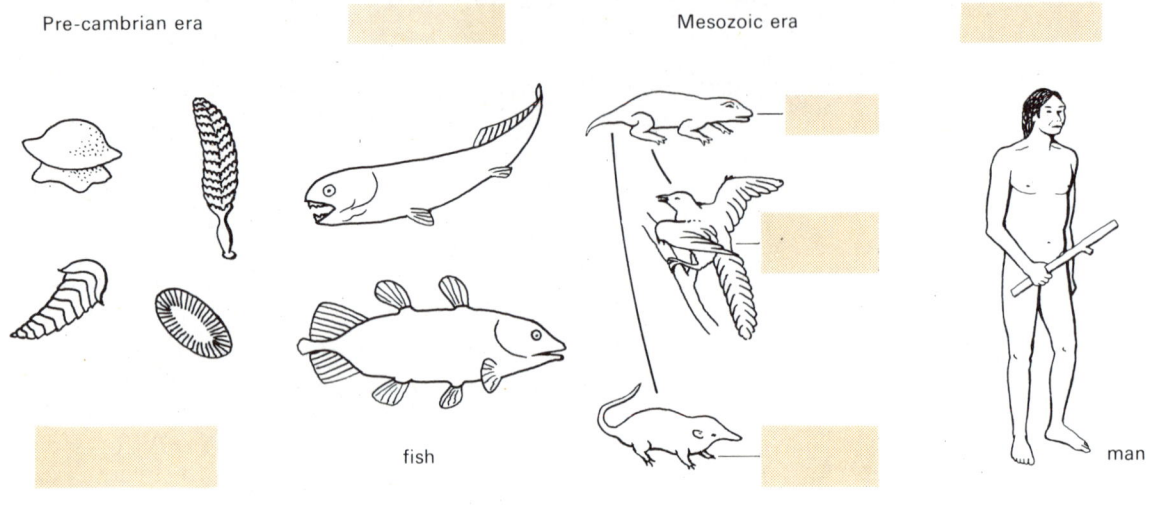

Pre-cambrian era

Mesozoic era

fish

man

SUMMARY

ERA .	EVENT
Pre-Cambrian era	Appearance of primitive organic structures
Palaeozoic era	Beginning of the age of fish
Mesozoic era	Development of reptiles Evolution of birds, mammals Disappearance of many reptiles
Cenozoic era	Appearance of man

STATEMENTS

At the beginning of the Pre-Cambrian era there was no life on earth.
Primitive organic structures appeared in the sea 3500 million years ago.
The age of fish began in the Palaeozoic era.
Reptiles developed during the Mesozoic era.
Some reptiles evolved into primitive birds. Other reptiles developed into
early mammals.
At the end of the Mesozoic era many reptiles disappeared. Man appeared
in the Cenozoic era.

Task 1

Label the diagram.

72

Steam engines

DIAGRAMS

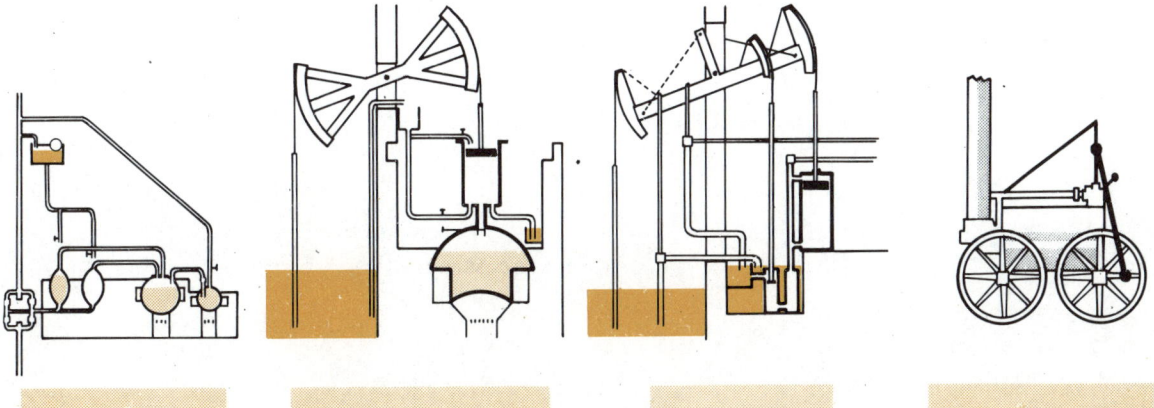

SUMMARY

16th century	first attempts to . . . . . .
	Savery's steam engine
	modification by . . . . . .
1760s	improved by . . . . . .

STATEMENTS

Attempts to make steam engines began in the 16th century.
In 1698 Thomas Savery built one of the first steam engines.
Steam was condensed in a vessel. Water was forced up into a cylinder.
In 1705 Newcomen modified Savery's steam engine.
In the 1760s James Watt improved Newcomen's design.
In the early 1800s Trevithick designed a successful high-pressure engine.

Task 2   Label the diagram.

Task 3   Complete the summary.

Part 2
Language study

Patterns 1   *Man appeared in the Cenozoic era.*
= Man appeared during the Cenozoic era.

He lived there from 1840 to 1850.
= He lived there for 10 years.

Task 4   Use the tables to complete the paragraphs.

THE VIKINGS
```
 800
 850
 870    arrival in Iceland                    ⎤ discovery and colonization
 900                                          ⎢   of many lands
 928    landing in Greenland                  ⎢ trade with China
 930    foundation of the Republic            ⎣ travel to many countries
           of Iceland
 950    discovery of North
           America
1000    colonization of North
           America
1100    disappearance from North
           America
```

The Vikings from Scandinavia were great explorers. During the ninth
and . . . . . . centuries they discovered and colonized . . . . . .   For . . . . . .
hundred years they travelled to . . . . . . and traded . . . . . .   They
arrived in Iceland in . . . . . . and in 928 they landed . . . . . .   In . . . . . .
the Republic . . . . . . was founded. Between 950 and 1000 they . . . . . .
North America. From . . . . . . to . . . . . . they . . . . . . North America. At the
beginning of the . . . . . . century they . . . . . . from North America.

19th CENTURY	Discovery by Maxwell of electromagnetic waves.
	First generation of electromagnetic waves by Hertz.
1895	Demonstration of a system of wireless communication by Marconi.
1899	Transmission of a radio signal from England to France.
1901 · December 12	Transmission of a radio signal across the Atlantic.

74

...... the nineteenth century Maxwell ...... electromagnetic waves.   ...... were first generated by .... demonstrated a system of ......   In 1899 Marconi transmitted ......   On December 12 ...... Marconi ......

Task 5   Correct these statements where necessary.
1   The Vikings arrived in Iceland in the ninth century.
2   The Republic of Iceland was founded in the eleventh century.
3   The Vikings discovered China during the tenth and eleventh centuries.
4   The Vikings were colonized by North America.
5   Maxwell generated electromagnetic waves in the nineteenth century.
6   The Atlantic was transmitted across a radio signal in 1901.
7   In 1895 a system of wireless communication was demonstrated by Hertz.
8   Before 1900 a radio signal was transmitted from England to France.

Patterns 2   *Reptiles developed. Birds appeared.*
= Reptiles developed. Then birds appeared.
= Reptiles developed. Next, birds appeared.
= Reptiles developed. After that, birds appeared.

Task 6   Number the statements in each group to show the correct order.

THE ORIGIN OF LIFE ON EARTH
a   Primitive organic structures appeared in the sea.
b   It began to cool.
c   The earth was a liquid ball.
d   It developed a solid crust.
e   Oceans were formed.

FOSSILS
f   The remains of the animal were preserved in this rock.
g   The soft parts were replaced by sediment.
h   The soft parts of the animal decayed.
i   An animal died.
j   The sediment was compressed into rock.

Task 7   Write each group of statements in Task 6 in the form of a paragraph. Use these words to show the sequence: *first; next; then; after that; finally.*

75

Patterns 3   *Many reptiles disappeared. Then man evolved.*
= After many reptiles disappeared, man evolved.
= Before man evolved, many reptiles disappeared.

Task 8   Put these statements in the correct order.
1   The Phoenicians used pictures to send messages.
2   The Greeks extended the alphabet of the Egyptians.
3   Primitive man developed a system of oral communication.
4   The Egyptians developed the first alphabet.
5   The Romans adopted many of the Greeks' signs.

Task 9   Complete these statements.
1   After primitive man ......, ...
2   ...... the Phoenicians ......, the Egyptians ......
3   ...... the Greeks ......, the Romans ......
4   Before the Phoenicians used pictures to send messages, ...
5   ...... the Egyptians ......, the Phoenicians ......

Part 3
Discourse study   **Chronological development**

Task 10   Read the passage and complete table 1.

THE EARTH BEFORE MAN
For about 4000 years there was no life on earth. Primitive organic
structures (such as bacteria and algae) appeared in the sea more than 3500
million years ago. The age of fish began in the mid Palaeozoic era, about
400 million years ago.

The Devonian period was a time of great topographical change.
Mountains were formed. The oceans moved. This movement exposed
mud, which was rich in organic materials. Vegetation grew and then the
first insects appeared. After insects developed, amphibians appeared.

Reptiles developed during the carboniferous period and became the
dominant form of life. Some reptiles evolved into primitive birds, others
into early mammals. At the end of the Mesozoic era the surface of the
earth broke up into separate land masses and many reptiles disappeared.
The first men appeared about 600000 years ago.

TABLE 1

TIME	EVENT
over 3500 million years ago	Appearance of . . . . . . and . . . . . .
. . . . . . ago	Beginning of the age of . . . . . .
Devonian	1 formation of . . . . . . 2 movement of . . . . . . 3 growth of . . . . . . 4 appearance of . . . . . . and . . . . . .
	Development of reptiles. Evolution into . . . . . . and . . . . . .
. . . . . . of the Mesozoic era	Breaking up of . . . . . . Disappearance of reptiles
	Appearance of man

Task 11   Match each event in table 2 to its corresponding time.

TABLE 2

TIME	EVENT
1 about 1500 2 18th century 3 1899–1903 4 1909 5 1938	a Bleriot flew from France to England b the Wright brothers developed an aircraft with an engine c the first jet aircraft was built d the Montgolfier brothers made hot-air balloons e Leonardo da Vinci designed aeroplanes and helicopters

Task 12   Use table 2 to complete this passage.

More than 450 years ago . . . . the Montgolfier brothers made hot-air balloons.   . . . . . . the Wright brothers developed an aircraft with an engine.   . . . . . . years later . . . . years ago . . . . . .

Historical description

Task 13 Read the passage and label the diagrams.

Attempts to make steam engines began in the sixteenth century. In 1698 Thomas Savery built one of the first steam engines. It was a simple pump with no moving parts. Steam was cooled and condensed in a vessel. As a result, a vacuum was formed and water was forced up into the cylinder.

In 1705 Newcomen modified Savery's steam engine. Newcomen's engine used a piston in a cylinder, but it had a serious design fault. The cylinder was alternately heated and cooled. The steam had to reheat the cylinder every time. A lot of heat was wasted.

In the 1760s James Watt improved Newcomen's design. The steam was condensed in a separate condenser. Consequently, the temperature of the cylinder did not change and heat was not wasted.

In the early 1800s Trevithick designed a successful high-pressure engine. After that, only minor modifications were made to the design of steam engines.

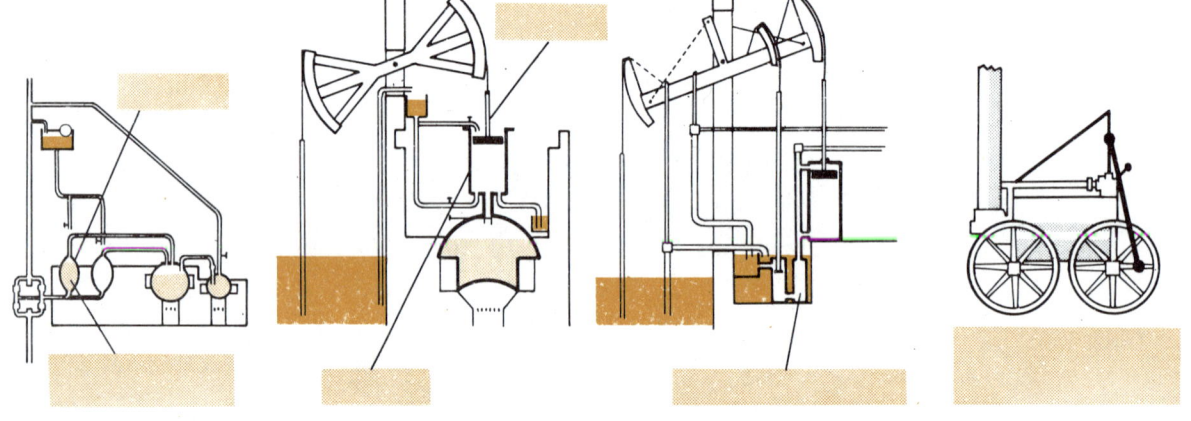

Task 14 Complete table 3.

TABLE 3

Savery's engine	1 Steam . . . . . . 2 . . . . . . condensed. 3 . . . . . . was formed. 4 . . . . . .
Newcomen's engine	The cylinder . . . . . . ∴ the steam . . . .
Watt's engine	The steam . . . . . . ∴ the temperature . . . .

Task 15 Use the pictures and table 4 to complete the passage.

Dimetrodon lived during the . . . . . .   It . . . . . . 4 short . . . . . .   On its back there was a . . . . . .   This membrane enabled it to . . . . . .   It ate . . . . . . and . . . . . . slowly.

Brontosaurus . . . . . . the Jurasic period. It . . . . . . a . . . . . . neck and tail. Its total . . . . . . 20 metres and it weighed . . . . . .   It . . . . . . vegetation and . . . . . . near water.

Brontosaurus

Dimetrodon

TABLE 4

Dimetrodon	Permian period carnivorous slow movement triangular membrane – control body temperature
Brontosaurus	Jurasic period herbivorous near water weight: about 40 tons

Part 4
Extension

Task 16   Read the passage and complete table 5.

ANCIENT EGYPT

Ancient Egypt consisted of the desert regions surrounding the Nile. This region was the centre of one of the great early civilizations. The civilization was based on cereal production. The soil near the river was very fertile. Drainage and irrigation necessitated large scale co-operative effort. Consequently, the growth of urban communities and central organization was stimulated.

After about 5000 BC the early Egyptians introduced the use of copper, the first writing, and sea-going ships. Before about 3200 BC Egypt was divided into two states. The two states were combined by a pharaoh named Menes. During the next thousand years the Egyptians developed a strong system of government. They began to build pyramids and temples and made magnificent works of art.

After a period of decline and anarchy there was a period of imperial expansion overseas between 1570 and 1075 BC. Later, Egypt was invaded and conquered many times and in 30 BC it became a Roman province. In AD 640 it was conquered by the Arabs at the battle of Heliopolis. It became a Muslim country.

TABLE 5

TIME	EVENT
	use of copper
	formation of one state
3200–......BC	development of a strong system of government
before	decline and anarchy
	imperial expansion
	invasion by Romans
	conquest by Arabs

Task 17   List the aspects of Egyptian civilization mentioned.

Task 18   Complete these statements.
1   ...... were grown near the Nile.
2   ...... were introduced by ......
3   The period of ...... expansion lasted for ...... years.
4   After the empire ...... Egypt ...... many times.
5   Drainage and ...... enabled ...... to grow.

Unit 10   Final review

Task 1 Read Part 1 of the passage and label the diagram.

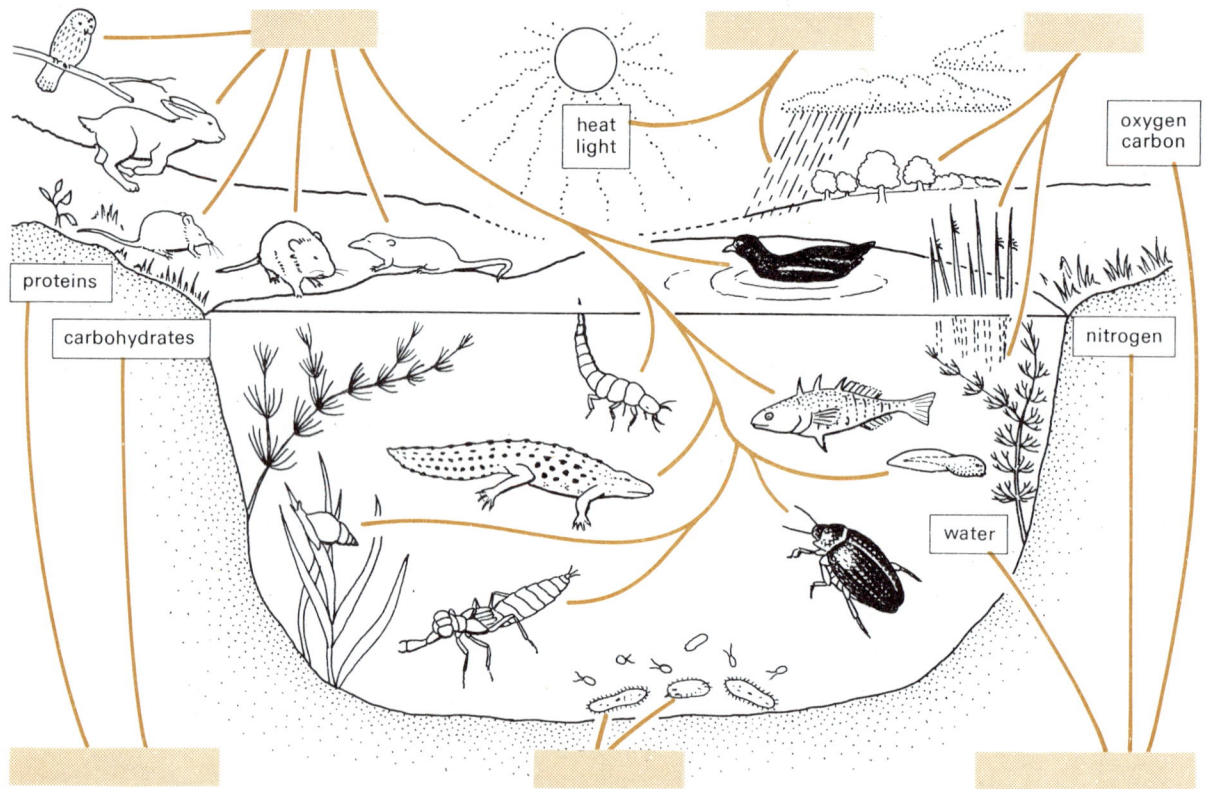

heat light

oxygen carbon

proteins

carbohydrates

nitrogen

water

ECOSYSTEMS

Part 1

An ecosystem consists of a number of living organisms and their physical environment. The living organisms and their non-living environment are interrelated and interact with each other. There is a flow of energy from the non-living organisms to the living organisms. There are a number of materials cycles – that is, exchanges of materials between living and non-living parts. When we study an ecosystem we can therefore analyse its components (the structure of the ecosystem) and we can analyse its processes (the functions in the ecosystem).

There are six major components in an ecosystem.

1   Inorganic substances such as carbon, nitrogen, oxygen, water, carbon dioxide etc.

2   Organic compounds such as proteins, carbohydrates etc. The organic and inorganic substances in an ecosystem regulate the work of the whole system.

82

3 Climate and other physical factors. Temperature, wind, light and rain are important physical factors. They affect all the processes in an ecosystem.

4 Producers. Only green plants are able to manufacture food from simple inorganic substances. In the process known as photosynthesis green plants in the light of the sun combine carbon dioxide and water and produce carbohydrates.

5 Consumers. Consumers obtain their energy from green plants. Herbivores, such as cows and sheep, eat green plants but do not eat other animals. They are called primary consumers. Carnivores, such as dogs and cats, feed on other animals and are called secondary consumers.

6 Decomposers, such as bacteria and fungi. Decomposers break down the tissues and excretions of other organisms. Bacteria break down the flesh of dead animals. Fungi break down plant material. They enable chemical substances to return to the physical environment.

Task 2   Complete table 1.

TABLE 1

COMPONENT	EXAMPLES	MAIN ACTIVITY
1	carbon nitrogen etc.	
2		
3		
4		manufacture food from inorganic substances
5 primary ......, ...		
6		

Task 3   Answer this question.

Why are decomposers important in an ecosystem?

Task 4   Read Part 2 and label the diagrams.

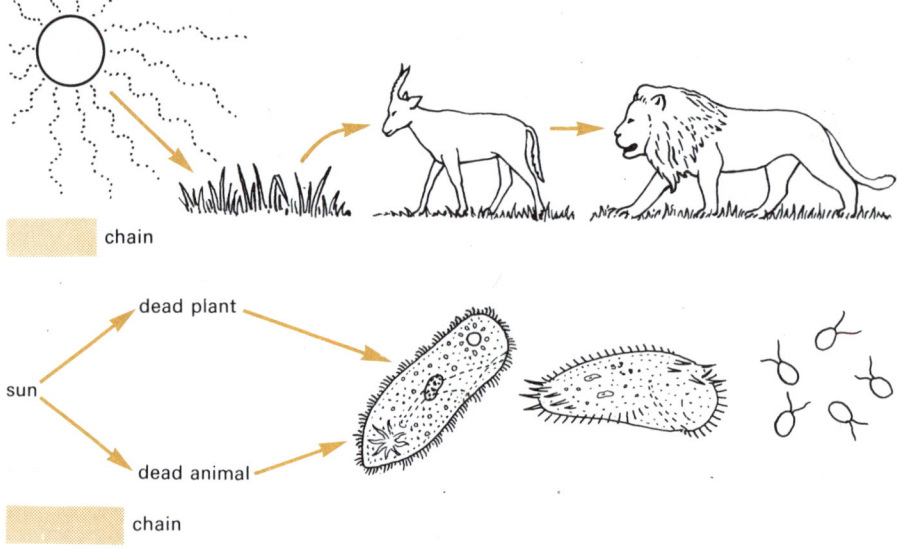

◻◻◻ chain

sun

dead plant

dead animal

◻◻◻ chain

Part 2

The main processes in ecosystems include: food chains, materials cycles, development and evolution.

FOOD CHAINS

The sun's energy travels through an ecosystem. The transfer of energy through an ecosystem by the producers, the consumers and the decomposers is called a food chain.

Green plants use the sun's energy to manufacture food. They are the first stage, or link, in the food chain. When an animal eats a green plant some of the sun's energy will be passed to the animal. The energy will be used for growth, for movement and other body processes. When a carnivore eats another animal, another transfer of energy is made.

In a predator chain, energy is transferred from the plant to the herbivore and from the herbivore to the carnivore. In a saprophyte chain the energy from the sun is transferred from dead plants and animals to micro-organisms.

Man occupies a position at or near the end of a food chain. Some food chains are long. For example, phytoplankton in the sea fix the sun's energy and are eaten by zooplankton. Zooplankton are eaten by small fish. Large fish feed on the small fish and are eaten by man. Other food chains are short. For example, cow's milk comes from a short food chain with two links.

Only a small percentage of the sun's energy is fixed by plants. In addition, 80–90% of the energy is lost at each link in the chain. Consequently, the input of energy at the end of a chain is only a small percentage of the energy output at the beginning of a chain. The amount of energy at the end of a chain will depend on the length of the chain. When the chain is short each plant provides a large amount of energy. When the chain is long each plant provides a small amount of energy. Consequently, one large animal at the end of a chain has to consume many small animals. Small animals have to consume a large number of plants. In this food pyramid one man has to obtain energy from a large number of other organisms.

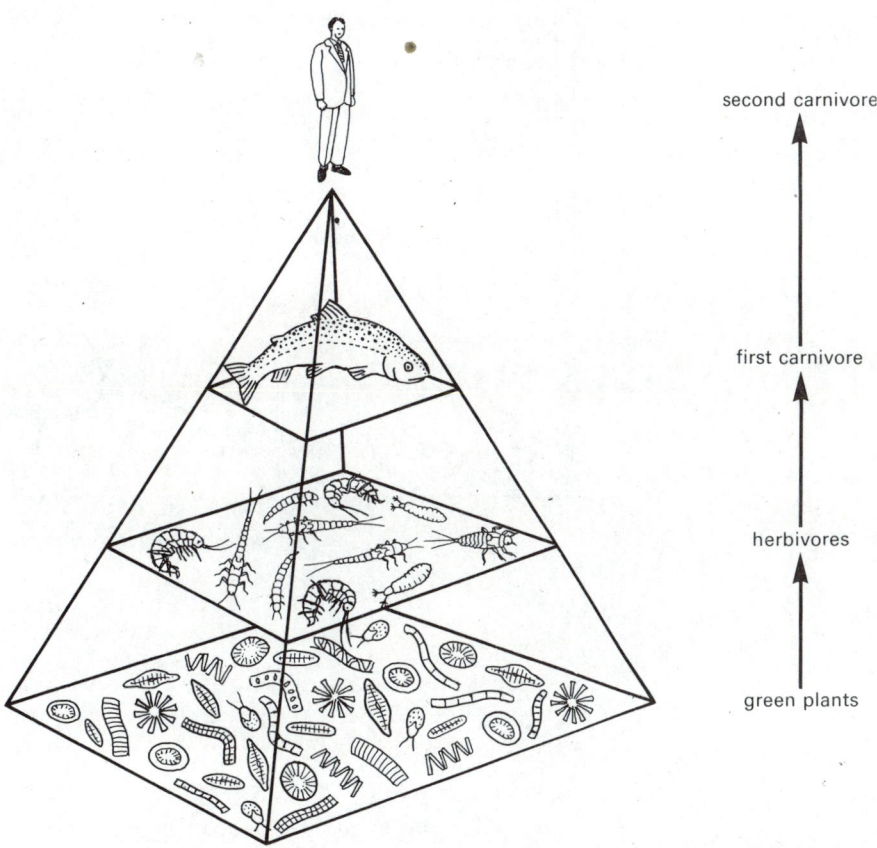

second carnivore

first carnivore

herbivores

green plants

Task 5   Draw two diagrams to show a long food chain and a short food chain.

Task 6

Answer these questions.
1   What is a food chain?
2   What is the first link in a food chain?
3   What is the second link in a predator chain?
4   What percentage of energy is transferred at each link?

Task 7

Read Part 3 and label the arrows to complete the diagram.

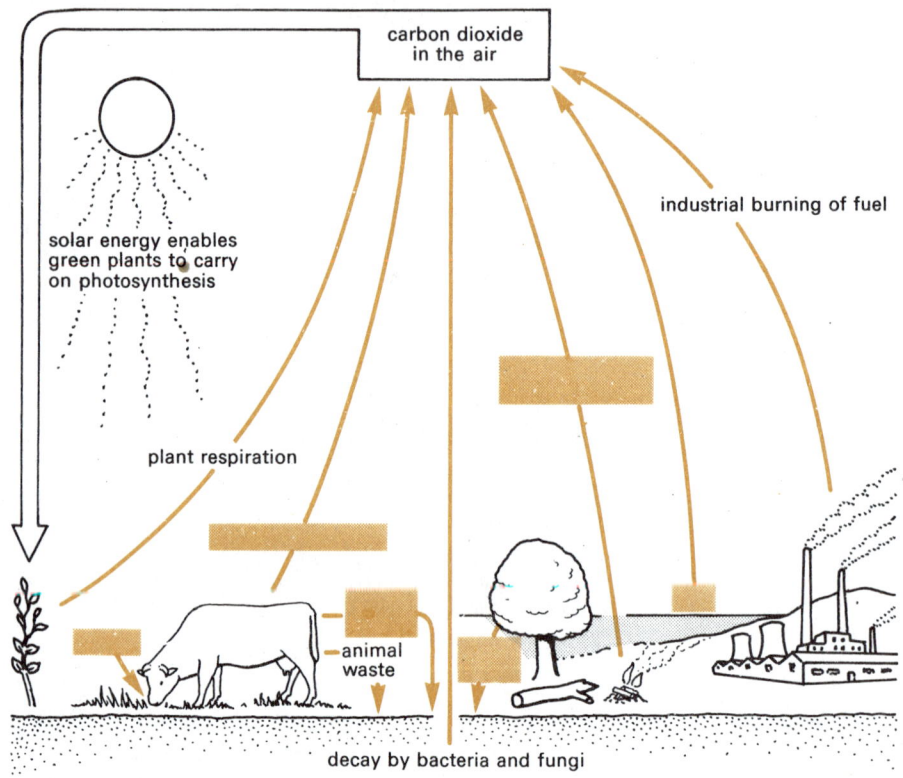

Part 3

MATERIALS CYCLES
Chemical substances move from the non-living environment to living things. They are then returned to the environment. There are cycles of nitrogen, carbon, oxygen, water and mineral salts.

THE CARBON CYCLE
Carbon dioxide exists in the atmosphere and in water. In photosynthesis plants take in carbon dioxide from the air. The carbon is converted into sugar. The sugar provides energy for the plant. Animals eat the plants

and carbon is passed from the plants to the animals. Carbon is returned to the atmosphere in several ways:

1   Respiration of all living things. When animals breathe out they return carbon dioxide to the air. When animals and plants die they provide food for bacteria and fungi. The food is used by bacteria and fungi in their respiration. The respiration also releases carbon dioxide.
2   When fuels such as coal and wood burn carbon dioxide is produced and enters the atmosphere.
3   Carbon dioxide is lost from the sea into the air.

Task 8

Read Part 4 and complete the table.

Part 4

DEVELOPMENT AND EVOLUTION

An ecosystem exists in a state of equilibrium. It can support a certain number of plants and animals of different species. When the population of one animal increases, there will be a change in the ecosystem. There will not be enough food and water for all the animals. Consequently, some will die. The system will return to its state of equilibrium. The ecosystem regulates itself in the same way as a thermostat regulates the temperature in a heating system.

Ecosystems are not static – they change all the time. Plants and animals are able to adapt to changes in the physical environment. It is possible to predict changes. For example, when fire destroys the vegetation in a region, there will be certain changes. First grass and some flowers will grow. Then insects will appear. The wind will blow the seeds of small trees. These trees will grow and birds will appear. As the trees grow, the grass will disappear and a dense forest will develop. Some trees cannot live in a dense forest and will die. Other trees will develop and a community of birds and animals will live in the forest.

During long periods of time ecosystems evolve. The evolution of an ecosystem is caused by factors inside and outside it. Consider the evolution of the atmosphere. When life began on earth, the atmosphere contained nitrogen, hydrogen and other gases but no oxygen. There was no ozone in the atmosphere. Consequently, the sun's rays prevented life from developing on land. The first living organisms developed under the sea. After the evolution of photosynthesis, the oxygen in the atmosphere increased and life expanded. Complex living organisms developed. As the oxygen in the atmosphere increased, a layer of ozone was formed. Life was then possible on the surface of the earth. Life on earth depends on the equilibrium of the atmosphere. There is now a danger that man-made pollution will destroy the equilibrium.

GROWTH OF A . . . . . .

1   . . . . . . of grass and some flowers.
2   Appearance of . . . . . .
3   Growth of . . . . . .
4   . . . . . of birds.
5   Development of . . . . . birds and animals.

Task 9

Complete this table.

Causes ——————————————————————————————→ Effects

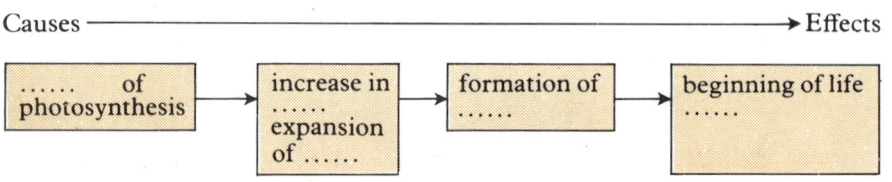

Task 10

Answer this question.

Why is man-made pollution a danger?

Acknowledgements

The publishers would like to thank the following for their assistance and co-operation in developing Reading and Thinking in English for publication:

The University of the Andes, Bogotá, Colombia

The British Council in London and Bogotá

The University of London Institute of Education.

Early versions of materials for this book and other titles in the series were used in trial teaching by the following Colombian universities:

Universidad Nacional, Bogotá

Universidad Social Católica de la Salle, Bogotá

Universidad Pedagógica y Tecnológica de Colombia, Tunja

Universidad del Norte, Barranquilla

Universidad del Valle, Cali

Universidad Pedagógica, Bogotá

Illustrations on pages 7, 8 (bottom), 14, 17, 20 (bottom), 22, 26, 29, 42, 45, 46, 47, 53, 58, 61, 63, 64, 66, 67, 68, 72, 79, 82, 84 (both), 85 and 86 are by Derek Whiteley.

The publishers would like to thank the following for permission to base a number of illustrations on original drawings from the following sources:

L. J. Campbell and R. J. Carlton Editors, *Common Core Science*, Routledge and K. Paul © 1969.
Adapted as figures, pp. 6, 30, 53, 56, 60.

C. D. Gould, *Focus on Biology*, Wheaton © 1976.
Adapted as figures, pp. 26, 85, 86.

P. J. Kenway Editor, *Windridge General Science*, Schofield & Sims © 1977.
Adapted as figures, pp. 1, 29, 53, 54, 63, 68.

R. J. Wyatt Editor, *Cars: Macdonald Visual Library*, © 1971.
Adapted as figure p. 34.

Although every effort has been made to trace copyright holders, this has proved impossible in some cases. If any copyright holders incorrectly acknowledged will contact the publisher, corrections will be made in future editions.